NURSING RESEARCH:
The Application of Qualitative Approaches

Nursing Research

The Application of Qualitative Approaches

Peggy Anne Field & Janice M. Morse

AN ASPEN PUBLICATION®
Aspen Publishers, Inc.
Royal Tunbridge Wells
Rockville, Maryland
Aspen Publishers, Inc.
1985

Library of Congress Cataloging in Publication Data

Field, Peggy-Anne.
    Nursing research.

    "An Aspen publication."
    Bibliography: p. 141
    Includes indexes.
    1. Nursing — Research — Methodology. I. Morse,
Janice M. II. Title. [DNLM: 1. Nursing. 2. Research —
nurses' instruction. 3. Research — standards — nurses'
instruction. WY 20.5 F455 q]
RT81.5.F54   1985   610.73'072   85-13378
ISBN 0-87189-237-5

CONTENTS

TABLES AND FIGURES

Tables

Figures

PREFACE

The authors' purpose in writing this book was to provide a pragmatic guide for the graduate student or the nurse undertaking a first qualitative research study. It is intended to provide guidance and information for those researchers who wish to use qualitative approaches. Some of the discussion will also be of considerable value for the quantitative researcher. Writing a proposal, for example, contains many similarities for both the qualitative and quantitative researcher. The pitfalls described in relation to gaining entry to an institution hold for most types of research that require access to human subjects. Thus, while the book is written for those who wish to undertake qualitative research, it also contains information valuable to any nurse-researcher.

Clinical expertise is highly valued in nursing and frequently graduates of baccalaureate programs are encouraged to obtain clinical experience prior to beginning their graduate degree. The reason cited for this experience is the importance placed on the necessity for the graduate to readily identify 'meaningful' clinical problems for research. It is paradoxical that, when these same graduates select a clinical research problem, they often find that these research questions do not lend themselves elegantly to quantitative measures and are therefore not 'good research questions'.

It is the authors' belief that these clinical phenomena must be studied and that they are researchable questions if the right approach is selected. As qualitative research methods have been less commonly used in nursing research, educational courses have not been widely available for teaching students this approach. A shortage of nurse researchers prepared in qualitative methods has also contributed to the lack of nursing literature dealing with the procedures used in gathering and analyzing data.

When a course in qualitative research in nursing has been taught it has been necessary to use literature from other fields. Recently articles on aspects of qualitative research methods have been published, but these resources are scattered and frequently are narrow in focus, so missing the interrelatedness needed to understand the qualitative approach. This book has been developed in response to this perceived need.

In a book of this size it is not possible to provide comprehensive coverage of all topics. To compensate for this, a list of library resources is provided throughout the text and these references are supplemented by an extensive bibliography. The authors are indebted to Dr. Lizbeth Hockey who read and critiqued the original manuscript. Her enthusiasm and excitement regarding the importance of nursing research is well known. We are also indebted to Dr. Myer Horowitz for his careful and constructive critique. Within our own faculty we would like to thank Dr. Jannetta MacPhail for her continued encouragement, support and interest, Miss Patricia Hayes and Dr. Shirley Stinson for their valuable comments on early drafts of the manuscript. Assistance was also provided by those who read and critiqued our work, Iris Campbell, Jennifer English, Sharon Morgan, and Suzanne Tylko. The two most arduous tasks in completing the manuscript were undertaken by Robert Morse, who painstakingly edited the book while Karen Williams checked the format for the references and bibliography. We also wish to thank our typist, Tom Hall.

Finally, the writing of this book was made possible by a McCalla Professorship Award from the University of Alberta to Dr. Peggy-Anne Field and by the National Health Research and Development Program through a National Health Research Scholar Award to Dr. Janice Morse.

Edmonton, Alberta   Peggy-Anne Field
1985   Janice M. Morse

AUTHORS

Peggy-Anne Field RN, SCM, BScN, MN, PhD

Dr. Field is a Professor at the Faculty of Nursing, University of Alberta. She has published in the area of maternity nursing, menstrual disorders and qualitative research. She has conducted research on such diverse topics as: skills validation for maternity nurses; patient satisfaction with nursing care; helping the grieving mother; evaluation of graduates and community nurses' perspectives of nursing. Her interests include education for maternity nursing; nurse-midwifery; caregiving behaviour of nurses and ethnography and her major focus for her clinical expertise is maternal-newborn nursing. Dr. Field currently holds a McCalla Research Professorship at the University of Alberta.

Janice M. Morse RN, BS, MS, MA, PhD (Nursing), PhD (Anthropology)

Dr. Morse is an associate professor at the Faculty of Nursing, University of Alberta, an associate clinical nurse researcher for the University of Alberta Hospitals, and a Canadian National Health and Research Development research scholar. Her major interests are in the areas of culture and health and qualitative and quantitative research methods, and her clinical interest is transcultural nursing. She has conducted research on such topics as cultural response to pain, childbirth, infant feeding, menarche and patient falls and conducted research with the Amish in Pennsylvania, the Cree Indians in Canada and with the Fijians and Fiji-Indians in Fiji.

Chapter One

APPROACHES TO THEORY DEVELOPMENT

There are presently two major complementary approaches to research. These are known as the quantitative and qualitative methods. Unfortunately, rather than developing skills in both fields and selectively utilizing an approach best suited to their problem, researchers often decide to restrict their choice of methodology to either qualitative or quantitative approaches. Furthermore, some researchers are spending extraordinary amounts of energy justifying their preference for either qualitative or quantitative methods and pointing out the deficiencies of the other approach.

The origin of this unfortunate schism is not entirely clear. Perhaps it has risen from the perception of quantitative researchers, who, not understanding the epistemological perspective of qualitative research, perceive the qualitative researcher to be violating the rules of research methodology. Or perhaps it extends from the frustration of qualitative researchers attempting to get proposals approved by committees that use only quantitative criteria. Nevertheless, unless researchers can appreciate the strengths and the unique contribution each approach can make to the common cause (which, in nursing, is the improvement of patient care), we will all be losers. An examination of the weaknesses or shortcomings, or a discussion of the criticisms of researchers espousing one approach or the other will not be the focus of this chapter. Rather this chapter will be directed toward an examination of the strengths of quantitative and qualitative research and their contributions to nursing knowledge.

In nursing the primary purpose of both qualitative and quantitative research is the same: to develop nursing knowledge. However, at the most basic level, the differences in qualitative and quantitative approaches are apparent: qualitative approaches develop nursing theory inductively from the data, but only test those derived theories in a limited way. Although the theories are rich in meaning and may be relevant to the setting, it is frequently not known if they will be supported in other settings or with other populations. On the other hand, quantitative methods are primarily intended to test theories. The researcher works deductively by first identifying existing theory from the literature and obtaining definitions of the concepts. Hypothesized relationships are then proposed and the outcomes predicted. Data are collected and statistically analyzed, and on the basis of these results, the hypotheses are then accepted or rejected and the theory supported or modified accordingly.

From this description, the complementary nature of qualitative (theory developing, hypothesis generating) and quantitative (theory modifying, hypothesis testing) research is evident. Therefore, researchers must become skilled at using both approaches, wisely selecting a method according to the purpose of the research.

THE DEVELOPMENT OF THEORY

What is it that we mean by a 'theory'? Basically, a theory is a hunch, a guess, a speculation or an idea that may explain reality. Theories guide investigation both in qualitative and quantitative research, but generally provide guidance at a different stage in the research process. In qualitative, inductive research, the researcher examines the data for patterns and relationships, and then develops and tests hypotheses to generate theory or uses developed theories to explain the data. Quantitative researchers, on the other hand, work deductively by testing developed theory.

Where, then, does theory come from? Given that theory is not established fact, but rather the researcher's 'best guess' based on previous research, others' beliefs and values and personal values, then theory is a framework, a perception of reality, to be tested by research. Once it is tested and becomes 'fact', it is no longer a theory, but moves into the domain of knowledge or 'truth.' Theory becomes more and more believable as it is tested and retested. However, the most important point is that theory, whether obtained inductively or deductively, remains conjecture, but as it is tested becomes better confirmed. As it is derived from the researcher's present knowledge base and personal reality, theories are usually culturally tied to present paradigms (that is, the prevailing thought in a specific discipline). Therefore, theories are usually in agreement, rather than disagreement, with current trends. This aspect of research is currently receiving criticism (for example see Feyerabend, 1978) as researchers tend to create and test hypotheses that, for personal practical reasons such as ease of publication, will be consistent with established theories. They are more likely to select hypotheses that will be supported and will be statistically significant rather than to disagree with current thought and risk statistical insignificance. Therefore, extensive and important theories may continue to be used for prolonged periods of time (and be 'confirmed' by research), yet, in essence be totally and completely wrong.

These 'errors' are most evident historically. The intense debate in the 1930's on the relationship between race and I.Q. (Brace, Gamble and Bond, 1971), or the 'diseases' perceived to be caused by masturbation in the late nineteenth century (Engelhardt, 1978) are excellent examples of how current values shape theory which were supported, albeit invalidly, by research.

Unfortunately, this trap for researchers and theoreticians continues today. Theory, derived inductively because it is derived from reality, is unlikely to be a product of the researcher's cultural reality or a distortion of the 'truth', although present day values or personal biases are always a threat to validity.

The first step in becoming a researcher is to develop an acute sensitivity to the imbedded values and assumptions in society and in present day theories and research, and an acute self-awareness of one's own personal values, perspectives and biases. This task is difficult, as many of these values are implicit, and not easily recognized until contrasted or challenged by a different norm or set of values. These challenges are most easily identified when the rescarcher is exposed to another culture, and for this reason anthropologists traditionally work cross-culturally.

COMPONENTS OF THEORY

The most common terms associated with theory development are concept, construct and conceptual framework. Articles and textbooks use a variety of definitions which frequently contradict one another. For clarity these terms will be defined as they are used in this book.

Theory

Theory, to expand on the definition given earlier, is the researcher's perception of reality in which constructs and concepts are identified and relationships are proposed or predictions made. It is a systematic explanation of an event. Theory can be developed by inductive or deductive modes of thinking or it may be arrived at through a combination of inductive and deductive thinking, as proposed by Glaser and Strauss in their discussion of grounded theory (Glaser and Strauss, 1967; Glaser, 1978).

Concept

A concept is a term to which meaning has been attached through formal definition or by common usage (Diers, 1979, p.69). Concepts may be abstract, such as health, hope, anxiety or pain, or may be concrete. Concrete concepts are generally observable, such as asepsis, electrolyte imbalance, or compliance. Thus, 'bonding' may be considered an abstract concept, but a corresponding concrete concept may be 'maternal-newborn interaction', where specific observable behaviours between mother and child can be identified.

Construct

A construct may consist of several concepts. For example, the construct of caring may include such concepts as assistive, supportive or facilitative acts (Leininger, 1981). Social class may be a construct that contains the concepts of education, income and employment.

Conceptual Framework

A conceptual framework is a theoretical model that the researcher has developed to show the relationship among constructs and/or concepts for that particular study. In quantitative research it may be a summary of the rationale for conducting the study derived from the literature review. It is often used as a plan for the measurement of the variables in quantitative deductive research.

Variable

Variables are logical groupings of attributes (Babbie, 1983, p. 21). They are the measurable characteristics within a concept. For example, variables used to measure pain may be physiological indices of pulse, blood pressure, galvanic skin response, or they may be a group of psychological attributes (such as fear, anxiety). Measures to assess these variables are designed to rate or quantify an amount of pain experienced.

TYPES OF THEORY

Deductive Theory

Deduction means to infer from what has preceded, in research one therefore draws from previous knowledge in order to deduce potential relationships. Reasoning is the facility of deducing unknown truths from principles that are already known. It is on this premise of logical inference that the scientific paradigm for research has been built.

Kuhn (1962) has suggested that theories compete with one another for attention and that tensions ultimately arise between competing paradigms. Deductive theory, building as it does on previous knowledge and research, is less likely to disturb the prevailing paradigm unless competing tensions become strong. In the nursing field, the work of Klaus and Kennel on bonding (1976) was adopted by researchers to provide the conceptual framework for considerable further research. This later research assumed the correctness of Klaus and Kennel's findings and hypotheses were generated based on their studies. It is only recently that contradictions in the later findings of their studies have led to a reaction to the original theory of bonding (Elliott, 1983).

In most deductive studies hypotheses are generated from the researcher's knowledge of previous studies, from library research and from intuitive knowledge of the phenomena. The general knowledge in the field is used to generate hypotheses by demonstrating relationships and testing the predictive value of specific variables. The problem is that when one is dealing with human behaviour, if it is studied out of context, (such as in a laboratory), many of the related variables are lost. Thus generalizations from findings may not apply outside the experimental situation. An excellent example of this is provided by pain research. Many findings of studies conducted in the laboratory have not been confirmed in the clinical setting (Chapman, 1976).

Deductive theory is most valuable when the researcher has clearly identified constructs and concepts with which to work. This situation is most likely when the relationships to be tested have been previously demonstrated and there has already been considerable research conducted in the area. For example, in physiological research these principles frequently hold true, but this is less often the case in behavioural research where the data are more subjective.

In deductive theory the starting point is a set of concepts or a conceptual scheme. Some of the concepts will be descriptive, serving to show what the theory is about (for examples, health, hope, support). Other concepts will be operative, such as the degree of hope, or the strength of support. The theory will then consist of a set of propositions each stating a relationship between at least two of the properties, such as the 'degree of hope varies with the strength of the support system'. Mathematical symbols may be used to represent the variables. A set of propositions forms a calculus, such that a given proposition can be said to be derived or deduced from one or two earlier propositions. Propositions so derived are said to be explained. This is logical deduction in its most simplistic form. A deductive system also provides grounds for prediction or prescription. As theory is not fact, it is always open to new input which may change or modify it. However, prevailing theories may inhibit thinking which can blind the researcher to potential inaccuracies. The previous example of the problems related to the theory of bonding is an example of how this occurs.

Inductive Theory
Inductive theory is directed toward bringing knowledge into view. It is generally descriptive, naming phenomena and positing relationships. It

does not test association or predict future trends. The goal of the researcher
is to identify patterns or commonalities by inference from examination of
specific instances or events. The thought processes move from specific
ideas to more generalized ideas that result in the identification of concepts
and potential relationships. When the purpose is to understand the setting
or the events, analytic induction is an essential aspect of research. The
process involves identifying variables in order to generate theory. In
examining phenomena concepts are defined and tentative causes and
relationships are hypothesized. In practice the researcher alternates back
and forth between cause and definition and as understanding increases,
the definitions, hypotheses and developing theory are modified. Closure
of the concept is achieved when the relationship between the cause and
the definition is understood and theory developed. Denzin (1978) notes
that once the concepts become evident from the data then the task is
complete.

   In nursing, inductive theory building has been used by Leininger
(1981, p. 142) to develop a taxonomy of caring. It has also been used by
Larsen (1984) to demonstrate the career development of selected nurses
with earned doctoral degrees. Larsen identified the social structure of
careers, then compared the women's career patterns to Levinson's model
of male career development. She identified social structures rather than
attempting to make the structure fit the predetermined organizational
chart. The comparison followed the analysis phase of the research.

Grounded Theory
Grounded theory, as described by Glaser and Strauss (1967), is one
approach to the development of inductive theory, although both inductive
and deductive thinking are used in the process. They argue that if one
conceptualizes from the data, and if data have been accurately recorded,
then the constructs and categories must arise fitting the data. Theory
grounded in reality must provide an explanation of events as they occur
and thus is less likely to be invalidated by prevailing paradigms.

   At the time that grounded theory developed, it was observed that
social research focussed mainly on the verification of theory. It was
further argued that there was a prior step that was being neglected. This
step was the discovery of concepts and hypotheses relevant to the area
being researched. Given the state of nursing theory it would be legitimate
to argue that generation of theory is more critical than theory testing to the
development of nursing knowledge at this time. Grounded theory, as a
methodological approach to research, has utility for nurse-researchers
who are attempting to identify unknown or unclear phenomena.

   Grounded theory is: 'the discovery of theory from data systematically obtained from social research' (Glaser and Strauss, 1967, p. 2). Theory is linked to the data and is therefore valid. The likelihood of grounded theory being completely rejected or replaced by other theory is minimal, however it may require modification as reality changes over time. Deriving grounded theory is time-consuming and involves the study of a substantial quantity of data. Generating a theory from data means that hypotheses and concepts are searched out from the data in the course of research. However, the source of certain ideas, or even models, may also come from sources other than the data, but these are used as explanations after the preliminary theories are derived.

The value of grounded theory is in the realm of naming concepts and identifying their characteristics. When Glaser and Strauss (1966) studied patients dying in hospital they identified what they called 'awareness contexts'. They described four types of awareness of dying which are either shared or not shared by those around the patient.

While grounded theory was developed for sociological research it has obvious utility for nursing research. The current state of underlying theory development in relation to research questions of relevance to nurses require that more attention be paid to the development of concepts and the reality of the context in which they occur.

LEVELS OF THEORY

Levels of theory have been classified in many ways. One common distinction is that between grand theory and middle-range theory (Pelto and Pelto, 1978, p. 251). Grand theory attempts to explain a broad generalized phenomenon. As a consequence the constructs tend to be abstract but the power of explanation is increased. Middle-range (or mid-range) theory entails the use of more specific constructs and is of lower order. At this level the power of explanation is more focussed than in grand theory. In nursing the models proposed by Orem (1980) and Roy (1976) would be considered mid-range theory. For the purpose of this book the focus will be on levels of theory that are addressed by the research questions selected and approaches used by the qualitative researcher, which entail low-order propositions and hypotheses and middle-range theory.

In a professional discipline research must eventually produce knowledge in a form that can be used to improve the practice of that profession. Answers to research questions form the basis of theory and of nursing knowledge insofar as critical concepts and constructs are identified and demonstrated. It may be descriptive, prescriptive or predictive in nature. Different kinds of theory are used for different purposes but all theory has an intrinsic purpose.

Dickoff and James (1968) make a useful distinction among levels of theory by discussing factor-isolating, factor-relating, situation-relating and situation-producing theory. The questions raised in developing factor-isolating or factor-relating theory can best be addressed by qualitative methodology, whereas situation-relating (predictive) theory and situation-producing (prescriptive) theory raise questions that are more appropriately addressed through experimental, quantitative approaches. Studies based on research questions that relate to the first two levels of theory development will be discussed.

Factor-Isolating or Naming Theory
Factor-isolating theory is the most basic kind of descriptive theory. At this level of theory development factors are isolated and given names or conceptual handles that provide meaning in abstract terms to observable real-world phenomena (Diers, 1979). A recent example of naming theory is Morse's (1983) work on 'health definition' among an indigent population in an urban Canadian setting. Morse developed a lay model of health from concepts and propositions that expressed relationships between bodily and psychological well-being from holistic views of health that the subjects themselves held. Aamodt's (1981) work with Norwegian-American women identified categories such as 'working or acceptance', 'neighbouring' and 'keeping busy.' This naming process is a first step in developing a concept that can be used by nurses to help them understand the people for whom they are providing care. Gotlieb (1981) used a factor-isolating approach to identify the types of interventions nurses used in working with clients in health related situations. She identified the client tasks and the nurse's role across the four phases of the nursing process. She was able to categorize and order the nurse and client behaviours and relate them to the phases of nursing process. Field (1982), in a concurrent study of the same population, identified the phases of care-seeking behaviour engaged in by clients. Both these studies utilized a constant comparative approach in the development of the identified concepts.

Factor-isolating theory provides names or labels for things along with descriptive definitions for the terms employed, the concepts and categories identified are the theory. Factor-searching studies will utilize normative description, the naming theory being presented in the form of formal concepts with properties and formal definitions or categories. A construct regarding the meaning of becoming a dialysis patient was developed by Artinian (1983a). She identified three roles: the watcher role; the waiter role; and the emancipated role, and she further described the properties peculiar to each category.

Categories are the components of concepts that may be arranged in some sort of pattern or order and related to one underlying dimension. Thus factor-searching or naming studies are descriptive in nature and occur at the exploratory or formulative stage of theory development. An early and classic study of this nature is Whyte's (1955) study of *Street Corner Society*. This study provides rich description of a street gang and develops a framework of the social order of such a gang. For nursing, Carnevali (1966) explored patients' fears about pending surgery and developed a conceptualization of fear sources. Rosenthal, Marshall, McPherson and French (1980) categorized the behaviours of the patients who were a problem for nurses. They developed a taxonomy of behaviours that are ascribed to a 'problem' patient. This is a sound illustration of a factor-searching study. Current work on nursing diagnosis is also an example of taxonomy development.

Glaser and Strauss (1967) in their method of discovering 'grounded theory' have adapted a more formalized approach to factor-searching. Their intent is to develop concepts rather than to offer narrative description of an event or situation. The concepts are discussed and illustrated, that is, grounded in the data, so that the meaning can be understood by the reader.

Problems for factor-searching studies ask the question, 'What is this phenomenon?' Such questions occur when a significant problem for nursing is identified but when little is known about the topic or subject area. If the topic has previously never been addressed the problem itself may not be clear. Thus, research questions may start by being broad and general and may only become more focussed as the study progresses. A qualitative researcher may enter a setting with a topic for study, rather than a clearly delineated question. The question is defined and refined in the setting as the phenomena are isolated. The constraints and flexibility of studying the phenomena within the setting may also guide the development of the final research questions.

The second level of theory proposed by Dickoff and James (1968) is relation searching, the development of factor-relating theory. This research uses an exploratory descriptive approach.

Factor-Relating Theory

Diers (1979) uses Dickoff and James' work and develops categories to further identify the focus of factor-relating theory. She speaks of this level of theory as being situation-depicting or situation-describing, indicating that the level of theory makes connections among concepts and relates factors, rather than merely describing them. This level of theory is still descriptive in nature and the research is not designed to test the observed relationships but rather to discover if there are any relationships between the identified concept and other variables. Relation-searching research is based on the question, 'What is happening here?' (Diers, 1979, p. 125). Quarnstrom and Lindstrom (1983), in an exploratory descriptive study of grief reactions of the elderly to the loss of a significant other, discovered that health status, sex of the bereaved person and resources available to the bereaved appeared to influence adjustment. Their findings resulted in factor-relating theory regarding bereaved persons most likely to be at risk for 'pathological grief.'

Artinian (1983b) proposed a relationship between reciprocal support and hope in the child with a bone marrow transplant. This work built on earlier research by Thompson (1980) in the home setting in which reciprocal support had been identified as an important mechanism in family life. In the hospital non-reciprocal relationships with nurses occurred and this type of relationship was inadequate to help families maintain hope. The negative example strengthened the finding of the potential relationship between a therapeutic family relationship and hope. The researcher's conclusion was that such relationships presented the mechanism through which creative planning for an uncertain future could be achieved.

The relationships found in factor-relating theory are stated either as propositions or hypotheses. Because the descriptions in the theory are without time reference they depict a situation rather than establish relationships. Factor-relating theory can stand by itself as it can form the basis for situation-relating theory. In some nursing research, tests have been used in which the constructs and their relationships have not been clearly identified. As early nursing research frequently used methodology from other disciplines, which included constructs and relationships developed in laboratory settings which were not easily transferred into a nursing context, this reliance on other disciplines has meant that progress in developing situation-relating or situation-producing theory related to nursing has been slow. Carefully designed research at the level of factor-searching and relation-searching will provide a sound descriptive base of nursing and nursing practice. If one compares this research cross-culturally, commonalities across nursing will become evident and can be used to develop a more global nursing theory. Diers (1979) argues that activities of factor-naming and factor-relating theorists are those of discovery as opposed to activities whose purpose is to confirm or verify the existence of something already discovered and predicted, which occur in situation-relating or situation-producing theory.

THE PURPOSE OF QUALITATIVE RESEARCH

The previous sections have suggested that qualitative methods should be used when there is little known about a domain, when the investigator suspects that the present knowledge or theories may be biased, or when the research question pertains to understanding or describing a particular phenomenon or event about which little is known. Qualitative methods are particularly useful when describing a phenomenon from the emic perspective, that is, the perspective of the problem from the 'native's point of view' (Harris 1968). In nursing studies the emic perspective may be the perspective of the patient, nurse or relatives. Qualitative research is usually conducted in a naturalistic setting, so that the context in which the phenomenon occurs is considered to be a part of the phenomenon itself. Thus, no attempt is made by the researcher to place experimental controls upon the phenomenon being studied, or to control the 'extraneous' variables. Thus all aspects of the problem are explored, and the intervening variables arising from the context are considered a part of the problem. Using this approach the underlying assumptions and attitudes are examined, and the rationale for these are also elicited, within the context in which they occur. Germain's 1979 study of the cancer ward provides an excellent example of the necessity of understanding the contextual factors in order to understand the phenomena.

As previously mentioned, the qualitative approach to understanding, explaining and developing theory is inductive. This means that hypotheses and theories emerge from the data set while the data collection is in progress, and after data analysis has commenced. The researcher examines the data for descriptions, patterns, and hypothesized relationships between phenomena, then returns to the setting to collect data to test the hypotheses. Thus, the research is a *process* that builds theory inductively over a period of time, step by step. The theory fits the research setting and is relevant for that point in time only. These data may largely consist of transcriptions of interviews, observations of the setting and of the actors. Data of these kinds are meaningful to others, and considered 'rich' and 'deep'. However, these data are hard to manage for the purposes of analyzing and writing a report, as they can not be readily transformed into numeric codes for statistical manipulation. In this respect they are often said to be 'soft' data.

The qualitative research process can be exceedingly time-consuming, both for the collection and the analysis of data. In contrast to quantitative research, the number of subjects in the study is necessarily small and a random sample is not selected. Rather, the researcher selects 'informants' who are willing to talk and have established relationships of trust with the researcher or who are in 'key' positions and have a special knowledge of the phenomena for one reason or another.

THE PURPOSE OF QUANTITATIVE RESEARCH

Quantitative research, in contrast to qualitative research, seeks causes and facts from the etic or 'world view' perspective (Osborne, 1977). In this case the findings are based on the researcher's interpretations of the observed phenomena, rather than on the subjects' interpretations of events. Quantitative research looks for relationships between variables so that causality may be explained and accurate prediction becomes possible. The aim is to examine the experimental variables, while controlling the intervening variables that arise from the context. With this control over the effects of context the relationships between variables will be generalizable and predictive in all settings, at all times.

Quantitative researchers establish a theory identifying all constructs, concepts and hypotheses while preparing the proposal and before beginning data collection. These concepts are operationalized so that the hypotheses may be tested. Concerned with rigor and replication, the researcher ensures that the measurement instruments are reliable and valid. Data are then collected, numerically categorized and the relationships between the variables used to measure the concepts are established statistically, using 'hard' data. Bias is controlled by randomly selecting a large and representative sample from the total population. Structured instruments, such as rating scales, are frequently used to collect data, and are usually administered once, as it is assumed that reality is *stable* (that is, the variables measured will not change over time). The techniques for research design and analysis are prescribed *a priori* in the research proposal and there are acceptable, tested and appropriate written steps or guidelines to assist the researcher throughout the process. The goal of quantitative research is to test the theory deductively by supporting or not supporting hypotheses.

SELECTING A METHOD

In summary, one has available two distinctly different research approaches. These should be selectively and appropriately used according to the nature of the problem and what is known about the phenomena to be studied. Criticisms from other researchers are not appropriately targeted towards methodological paradigm preferences. Critics should assess the method used to see if it was justified and was appropriate to the problem. This applies to criticism of both qualitative and quantitative research.

The choice of method depends on a number of factors discussed below:

Nature of the Phenomena to be Described

The type of variables, or the nature of the question may indicate that either qualitative or quantitative methods would be more appropriate. For example, the purpose of the proposed study may be to examine the fears and anxieties of preoperative patients. Fear and anxiety can, to a considerable extent, be measured, reliably and validly, quantitatively, using standardized anxiety scales. Physiological measurements of stress may also be used, for example, by measuring heart rate, galvanic skin response or adrenocorticotropic hormones. Fear and anxiety may also be studied qualitatively by asking patients to describe their fears and feelings about impending surgery.

Consider the purpose of the study. Is the purpose to test the effectiveness of a nursing intervention designed to reduce preoperative stress? Or is it to learn about the nature of the patients' fears and anxieties? That is, are the patients afraid of the violation of their body boundaries, loss of control of their body during the anaesthetic, of pain, or of the unknown post-operative recovery period?

Answering the first question the quantitative researcher will make theoretical assumptions, or use past research on the anxieties of the preoperative patient, and using an experimental two-group design, measure the effectiveness of the nursing intervention by quantifying differences between the two groups. To answer the second question, the qualitative researcher will describe, in depth, the fears of the preoperative patient in order to 'know' the experience, and create a theory of factors contributing to preoperative fears and anxieties. Following this step the qualitative researcher may move into an experimental quantitative research study to test nursing measures which will reduce pre-operative stress.

Occasionally, the choice of qualitative or quantitative measurement will also depend on external resources, such as the expertise of the researcher. Available budget should not influence the selection of method, but may dictate the size of the project that can be undertaken. Researchers are frequently limited in their choice of research design by the knowledge of their mentor and by their own knowledge and they are unwilling to try a 'new' approach and 'new' methods.

Unfortunately, funding agencies are also reluctant to fund researchers who do not have a 'track record' using research methods in which they have not previously demonstrated their expertise. A limit on available research funds may also restrict the researcher's choice of methodology.

Qualitative research is comparatively expensive and time consuming compared to quantitative methods. It is also more difficult to utilize research assistants to conduct unstructured interviews and to assist with data analysis. The researcher must consider the threats to validity of the research when these constraints dictate the choice of methods and carefully consider the cost of such compromise.

The Maturity of the Concept

By 'maturity of the concept' we mean how much has already been investigated about the topic, or how much is known. If an extensive library search reveals that there is very little previous information about a research topic, then the topic is probably not developed enough to use quantitative methods, and an exploratory, descriptive study using qualitative methods should be conducted. For example, if the topic to be investigated is, perhaps, mothers' attitudes towards breastfeeding, there is probably enough literature available on the topic to conduct a quantitative study. But if the research question is: 'What is it like to breast-feed?', where the focus is on the mother's own experience, there is little information available in the literature on this important topic. Thus, a descriptive, qualitative study would be appropriate.

Another occasion in which qualitative methods may be appropriately used is when there is a lot of information available on a particular topic, but a content analysis of the literature reveals that the research is based on assumptions which are not verified or are possibly biased. An example, again from the breast-feeding research, is the assumption that, in order to maintain lactation, breasts must be emptied four-hourly during the day. This assumption could not be verified in the literature, and a qualitative, exploratory research did not support the assumption (Morse, Harrison and Prowse, 1984).

Therefore, qualitative research questions are probably exploratory, seeking to describe a situation or to understand a person or an event (i.e., 'What is...?' or 'How does...?' questions). If, however, the research question is stated as an hypothesis seeking to demonstrate a relationship between two or more variables, then enough is probably known about the variables to use quantitative methods.

Constraints/Confines from the Subjects or Setting

The next factors to consider when selecting methodology arise from characteristics of the subjects or the setting. Are the subjects literate, and, if so, what languages do they speak? Will they be able to read a quantitative questionnaire, and if so, is the questionnaire culturally biased? If, for cultural reasons, quantitative methods are not suitable, then some form of qualitative methods will be necessary. Who are the subjects? Are they elderly, disoriented persons, or infants? If so, an observational technique, such as ethology, may be more appropriately used than a qualitative interview technique or a quantitative questionnaire.

METHODOLOGICAL THREATS TO VALIDITY

As stated earlier, there is a most appropriate approach to use for each research question. While there are advantages to every method, so there are limitations. Using an inappropriate method to answer a research question may result in loss of generalizability, increased cost, and invalidity.

Perhaps the most common problem in the inappropriate use of method is the use of inductive research design and qualitative methods when a considerable amount is known about the topic. Alternatively, it is equally invalid to use deductive research design and quantitative methods when too little is known about the topic. In the first case, researchers develop a conceptual framework, and then analyze qualitative data according to the categories in the framework, rather than deriving the categories inductively from the data. Thus, the researcher loses the qualitative strength of validity, by 'forcing' reality to fit the framework. If the researcher 'knows' enough about the topic to be able to create a conceptual framework and identify variables, then the researcher should be using quantitative methods.

The second error is the use of deductive quantitative methods when little is known about the subject. Invalidity occurs when the researchers attempt to 'create' instruments from the literature or his/her own experience, rather than beginning with a qualitative study to assist with the definition of the concepts. Meaningless, incomplete or erroneous results may be obtained. Both of these problems will be further discussed in Chapter Six.

MIXING QUALITATIVE AND QUANTITATIVE METHODS

Is it possible to use both qualitative and quantitative methods in the same study? The answer is most definitely 'yes', and often the strongest research findings are in studies that utilize both methods. The mix can occur either sequentially or simultaneously.

Sequentially

Qualitative and quantitative methods may be used sequentially as the project develops, with qualitative methods used initially until the hypotheses emerge. At this stage hypotheses may be tested using appropriate quantitative methods on a larger sample. For example, when examining parturition pain in the Fijian and Fiji-Indian women, Morse (1981) used ethnographic interviews to understand the cultural context of childbirth. Then, to confirm hypotheses regarding differences in the amount of pain attributed to childbirth in each culture, the expected painfulness of parturition was measured using a psychological scale.

Simultaneously

Qualitative and quantitative methods may be used simultaneously to address the same problem. This technique is known as *triangulation* (Jick, 1979). Qualitative methods may be used to describe the affective aspects of the domain, while quantitative methods may be used to measure other variables. A questionnaire, for example, may contain both standardized psychological tests in addition to open-ended questions that must be analyzed qualitatively and that will permit more freedom in the individual's response. Morse and Doan (1984) used this technique when examining adolescents' response to menarche. Open-ended, short answer questions were used to elicit information on the girls' feelings towards their first period. However, the same 'test-package' contained a Likert Scale to measure attitudes toward menstruation, and psychological tests such as draw-a-person.

Hockey (1976, pp. 230-4) used structured interviews with some open-ended questions to collect data for a study of *Women in Nursing*, one objective of which was to examine job satisfaction. She developed and used a Likert scale to measure the job satisfaction of the subjects in the study. In this study individual scores on the highest scale were related to interview comments in order to construct descriptive profiles of nurses who scored high, medium and low on the scales.

Another way in which qualitative and quantitative methods may be used together is when the researcher wishes to use a quantitative research design using qualitative measurement. This is useful when some of the variables may not be suitable for quantification. For example, a researcher may wish to examine the effect of preparing parents for their child's surgery, and measuring the effectiveness of their care by using proxemic (spatial distance) behaviour as the independent variable. The hypothesis may be that, by encouraging parents to move close and comfort the child, despite the child's condition and the presence of equipment, the child will be less anxious post-operatively. As proxemic behaviour is a variable that is difficult to quantify, a qualitative measurement of parent-child personal space may be used in conjunction with other quantitative measures.

REFERENCES

Aamodt, A. (1981) "Neighbouring: Discovering Support Systems among Norwegian-American Women" in D. Messerschmidt (ed.) *Anthropologists at Home in North America*, Cambridge University Press, Cambridge.

Artinian, B.M. (1983a) 'Becoming a Dialysis Patient', in E. Hamrin (ed.), *Research: A Challenge for Practice*, Proceedings of the Workgroup of the European Nurse Researchers' First Open Conference, Uppsala, Sweden, pp. 146-9.

Artinian, B.M. (1983b) 'The Relationship Between Reciprocal Support and Hope in the Bone Marrow Transplant Child', in E. Hamrin (ed.), *Research: A Challenge for Practice*, Proceedings of the Workshop of the European Nurse Researchers' First Open Conference, Uppsala, Sweden, pp. 140-5.

Babbie, E. (1983) *The Practice of Social Research*, 3rd. edn., Wadsworth Publishing Company, Inc., Belmont, California.

Brace, C.L., Gamble, G.R. and Bond, J.T., (eds.) (1971) *Race and Intelligence: Anthropological Studies Number 8*, American Anthropological Association, Washington, D.C.

Carnevali, D. (1966) 'Preoperative Anxiety', *American Journal of Nursing*, 7, 1536-8.

Chapman, C.R. (1976) 'Measurement of Pain: Problems and Issues', *Advances in Pain Research and Therapy*, 1, 345.

Denzin, N.K. (1978) *Sociological Methods: A Sourcebook* 2nd edn., McGraw-Hill, New York.

Dickoff, J. and James, P. (1968) 'Researching Research's Role in Theory Development', *Nursing Research*, 17, 197-203.

Diers, D. (1979) *Research in Nursing Practice*, J.B. Lippincott, Philadelphia.

Elliott, M. Ruth (1983) 'Maternal Infant Bonding', *Canadian Nurse*, 79(8), 28-31.

Engelhardt, J.R. (1978) 'The Diseases of Masturbation: Values and the Concept of Disease', in J.W. Leavitt and R.L. Numbers (eds.), *Sickness and Health in America: Readings in the History of Medicine and Public Health*, Madison, University of Wisconsin Press, pp. 15-23.

Field, P.A. (1982) 'Client Care-Seeking Behaviour in a Community Setting', *Nursing Papers*, 14(1), 15-29.

Feyerabend, P. (1978) *Against Method*, Varo, London.

Germain, C.P. (1979) *The Cancer Unit: An Ethnography*, Nursing Resources Inc., Wakefield, Massachusetts.

Glaser, B.G. (1978) *Theoretical Sensitivity*, The Sociology Press, Mill Valley, California.

Glaser, B.G., and Strauss, A.L. (1966) *Awareness of Dying*, Aldine Publishing Company, Chicago.

Glaser, B.G., and Strauss, A.L. (1967) *The Discovery of Grounded Theory: Strategies for Qualitative Research*, Aldine Publishing Company, Chicago.

Gotlieb, L. (1981) 'Nursing Clients Toward Health: An Analysis of Nursing Interventions', *Nursing Papers*, 13(1), 24-31.

Harris, M. (1968) *The Rise of Anthropological Theory*, Thomas Y. Crowell, New York.

Hockey, L. (1976) *Women in Nursing, Hodder and Stoughton*, London.

Jick, T.D. (1979) 'Mixing Qualitative and Quantitative Methods: Triangulation in Action', *Administrative Science Quarterly*, 24, 602-11.

Klaus, M.H., and Kennel, J.H. (1976) *Parent Infant Bonding: The Impact of Early Separation or Loss on Family Development*, Mosby, St. Louis.

Kuhn, T.S. (1962) *The Structure of Scientific Revolutions*, University of Chicago Press, Chicago.

Larsen, J. (1984) *A Psychosocial Study of the Career Development of Selected Nurses with Earned Doctoral Degrees*, unpublished PhD thesis, Faculty of Education, University of Alberta, Edmonton, Canada.

Leininger, M. (1981) *Caring: An Essential Human Need*, Charles B. Slack, New Jersey.

Morse, J.M. (1981) Descriptive Analysis of Cultural Coping Mechanisms Utilized for the Reduction of Parturition Pain and Anxiety in Fiji, *Dissertation Abstracts International*, *42*(11), 4363B-4364B (University Microfilms No. 8202200).

Morse, J.M. (1983) *Understanding Lay Perceptions of Health*. Paper presented to the Council of Nursing and Anthropology at the XI International Congress of Anthropological and Ethnological Sciences, Vancouver, August 20-25.

Morse, J.M. and Doan, H. (1984) *Becoming a Woman: Analysis of Adolescents' Response to Menarche*. Paper presented to the Society for Applied Anthropology, Toronto, Ontario, March 14-18.

Morse, J.M., Harrison, M., and Prowse, M. (1984) *Minimal Breast-Feeding*, unpublished manuscript, University of Alberta, Edmonton, Alberta.

Orem, D.E. (1980) *Nursing: Concepts of Practice* 2nd edn., McGraw-Hill, New York.

Osborne, O. (1977). 'Emic-etic Issues in Nursing Research', *Communicating Nursing Research*, *9*, 373-80.

Pelto, P.J. and Pelto, G.H. (1978) *Anthropological Research: The Structure of Inquiry*, Cambridge University Press, Cambridge.

Quarnstrom, U., and Lindstrom, C. (1983) 'Grief Reaction Following Death of A Significant Other', in E. Hamrin (ed.), *Research: A Challenge for Practice*, Proceedings of the Workgroup of European Nurse Researchers First Open Conference, Uppsala, Sweden, pp. 133-9.

Rosenthal, C.J., Marshall, R.W., MacPherson, A.S., and French, S.E. (1980) *Nurses, Patients and Families*, Croom Helm, London.

Roy, Sister C. (1976) *Introduction to Nursing: An Adaptation Model*, Prentice-Hall, Englewood Cliffs, New Jersey.

Thompson, M. (1980) *An Investigation of the Relationship of Love, Mutuality, Freedom and Newness with the Perception of Hope in Patients with the Diagnosis of Cancer*, unpublished masters thesis, California State University, Los Angeles.

Whyte, W.F. (1955) *Street Corner Society* 2nd edn., University of Chicago Press, Chicago.

Chapter Two

QUALITATIVE APPROACHES: AN OVERVIEW

In the previous chapter, the rationale for a qualitative approach for nursing research was presented. In this chapter some of the approaches that may be used to examine phenomena from the emic perspective will be discussed.

DEFINITION OF TERMS

Many of the terms associated with qualitative research are specific to the field. Some of the key terms will now be identified and a definition given. Further terms may be found in the glossary. An understanding of the terminology is critical in understanding discussion or approaches to qualitative research.

Meaning

Meaning is the interpretation that informants place on the rules, issues and behaviour of the culture. The researcher must determine how the informant classifies information. The role of the researcher is to explain the meaning of the behaviour of a particular society, that is, to make the implicit knowledge explicit. The interpretation of the meaning is the informant's privilege, while the mode of explanation is the researcher's.

Common Sense Knowledge

Common sense knowledge has been described as the socially sanctioned facets of life in society that any bonafide member of the society knows and which are necessary for individuals to have in order to function in that society (Manis and Meltzer, 1978, p. 281). The knowledge may be implicit and unconscious, to be recognized only when the norms of behaviour are violated (for example, unspoken rules relating to personal space).

Understanding

Understanding is the discovery of the ways in which a culture accomplishes its human ends; why the approach works for the specific culture; and under what circumstances an approach works to achieve the desired ends. Understanding is the process of discovering the insider's perspective on the situation.

Definition of the Situation

Man constructs his own reality and responds as much or more to the meaning a situation has for him as to the objective features of a situation. The definition of a situation is the way a person interprets a given object or set of circumstances. An individual's definition of the situation and his/her attitude towards it will be similar to the definition and attitude of those who share common values and experiences (Tomovic, 1979, p. 43).

Process

Reciprocal influences provide energy for social interaction, whether between groups or people. The process may be the modes of interrelationships between groups, for example, the particular ways in which people become associated or disassociated.

Life-World Phenomena

The life-world is the world of everyday life; that is, the total sphere of experiences of an individual within the context of the objects, persons and events encountered in everyday life.

RESEARCH APPROACHES TO STUDYING EVERYDAY EXPERIENCES

The major approaches used in qualitative studies will now be examined. The commonality across all approaches is that society is explored from an emic point of view, trying to understand life from the perspective of the participants in the setting under study. The focus of the study is the everyday life-world phenomena of the informants, their satisfactions, disappointments, surprises and astonishments (Van Manen, 1978). Life events are not predictable and controllable and cannot be studied as if these parameters can be applied. To understand lived events one must consider societal processes. These include such things as the ways in which individuals come to agreements, what values they hold and how priorities are negotiated. The development of a study of the everyday life of society is often loosely called 'phenomenological' study. However, there are different ways in which scientists probe into life-world structures and these arise, in part, from a difference in the concerns about life experiences held by the social scientists.

The anthropological tradition has generated the approaches used in ethnography, ethnoscience and ethology, while the sociological tradition embraces ethnomethodology, analytic sociology and constitutive phenomenology. All these developments are descriptive analytical investigations of the world of human experience directing the focus of inquiry onto the structuring of activities within society. In contrast, in quantitative research the focus, when studying society, is on seeking variables and attempting to find lawful or correlational relationships between or amongst them.

Van Manen (1978) suggests that qualitative approaches can be organized by examining the depth of structure that is sought when selecting a particular approach. 'New ethnography', as described by Spradley and McCurdy (1972) utilizes ethnoscience techniques to examine the ways in which members of a culture name and classify the critical objects and their properties, or actors and their behaviours. Constitutive phenomenology, on the other hand, attempts to find the inner *meaning* of the essence of life-world phenomena from both the perspective of the informants and the culture as portrayed through the use of media, such as literature and poetry. An overview of the major approaches follows.

Ethnography

Ethnography is a generalized approach to developing concepts to understand human behaviours from an emic point of view. Multiple methods of data gathering may be used by the ethnographer. These include observation, interviews, geneaology, demography and life-histories. Some writers use the term 'ethnography' synonymously with participant observation, but this is incorrect. Participant observation may be employed by the ethnographer but is a mode of data collection as opposed to an approach to analytic enquiry itself. Participant observation may be used by any researcher engaged in qualitative research as one mode of data gathering. While participant observation and interviewing are the major modes of data collection in ethnography, they may, as previously mentioned, be supplemented by other techniques.

An ethnographic approach to the study of nursing is useful in that it allows the observer to view nursing in the context in which it occurs. Differences in perception between the researcher and the subjects can be clarified as they occur and as the researcher gains an understanding of the topic under study from the subject's perspective. That is, the knowledge gained is emic in nature, derived from the subject's view of the experience, rather than etic, responding to a view that is enforced, in part, by the researcher.

Ethnography is a means of gaining access to the health beliefs and practices of a culture. Such information is critical to enable nurses to provide care. Culture may be used in a broad ethnic sense in examining health beliefs, but it may also be used to examine the beliefs of subgroups in society, such as indigent populations or women. Aamodt (1982, p. 209) has identified several major contributions that ethnography can make to nursing research. She suggests that ethnography makes a contribution to nursing practice. Ethnography provides detailed descriptive data that can be used by practicing nurses to help them understand patients' behaviours. As the goal of ethnography is to examine the native's view, attention is directed to the view of the consumer rather than toward the view of the health care provider. Users of nursing care are a critical component of any theory of nursing and therefore their beliefs, values and understanding are essential in the development of nursing knowledge.

Ethnography is a profitable approach when nurses wish to learn more about groups whose members do not have the literary and language skills found in the middle-class nursing culture (Ragucci, 1972). The patients model of perceiving and interpreting health phenomena may be constructed from information provided by informants. This can be compared to the health model used by health care professionals. An understanding of the discrepancies between professional and patients' perceptions may result in better care.

An ethnographer asks the question: 'In what ways do members of society actively construct their social world'? (Spradley and McCurdy, 1972) Translated into a nursing study, the researchers might ask: 'What do nurses in a surgical unit see themselves as doing?' The researcher wants to find out what it is that one has to know in order to be accepted as a surgical nurse. What competencies must one have? What values must one hold to be accepted by other nurses in the group? Melia (1982) illustrates this process in her ethnographic study of student nurses. The students rapidly learn the values of the registered nurses in the hospital and are useful informants in distinguishing the differences between educational and service values. While educators may perceive the students as 'taking short cuts' the students perceive themselves as 'getting the work done.' For the students the service value of 'getting the work done' becomes the dominant value, as this is necessary for acceptance into the work culture.

Descriptive ethnography sets out to identify the social complexities that lie near the surface of a society. Ethnographic analysis moves deeper when the researcher wants to explain aspects of social patterns or observed conduct. This more analytically oriented ethnography has been called 'thick description' (Geertz, 1973). Thick description is an intepretive science which searches for meaning in a society. The general question behind thick description is: 'What social meanings and cultural biases lie at the base of social action?' Thus the researcher is concerned with the psychologically or culturally embedded norms which guide the actions of individuals in a specific culture. Field (1983) provides an example of descriptive ethnography in a study of the perspectives of four community health nurses and the way these perspectives influence their judgement and decisions. The study searches for the meaning of nursing for these four nurses as it is influenced by their particular setting.

Grounded Theory
Grounded theory can be considered as a form of ethnographic data analysis rather than as a separate qualitative approach. Grounded theory, unlike phenomenology, assumes the existence of a process. It involves both an inductive and deductive approach to theory construction in that constructs and concepts are grounded in the data and hypotheses are tested as they arise from the research.

Nurses have been active in the use of grounded theory. One of the earliest studies was Quint's (1967) report on 'The Nurse and the Dying Patient.' Fagerhaugh and Strauss (1977) developed a theory related to the politics of pain management in the hospital setting. Stern (1978) used the approach to examine affiliation in step-father families. More recently, Antle-May (1980) used grounded theory to examine the development of fathering behaviour, a subject that had been totally neglected in the literature until the last few years. In all these areas the knowledge base in the subject area was sparse and the researchers developed and tested propositions and hypotheses based on their observations and interview data. The resulting theory offers an explanation of the behaviours of patients and professionals and provides a base for identifying strengths and weaknesses in nursing practice. In the case of Stern's and Antle-May's studies the developing theories provide a base from which nursing interventions can be identified.

Ethnology
Ethnology is a special application of ethnography, in which the researcher develops theories of culture and society rather than focussing on individuals in the setting. It is used to compare and contrast cultures. Ethnology differs from ethnography in its goals, rather than in the methods used. Ethnology involves the cross-cultural comparison of norms and values along with a description of physical objects used by the cultures.

In nursing, the way knowledge is transmitted, the formal and informal rules governing the way nursing care is provided and the technology and equipment used in the provision of care would all be a part of the culture. Soares' (1978) study of nursing in an intensive care unit utilizes this type of framework to describe the culture of the unit. If this study were extended to examine other similar units, then ethnological methods could

be applied to examine cultural similarities and differences. All comparative work depends on thorough and precise ethnographic description.

Ethology

Ethology is an observational technique in which behaviours are recorded,
coded, categorized and analyzed. Ethology was developed and adapted
from research on animal behaviour in an attempt to accurately record,
describe and derive explanations for the behaviours (Gould, 1982).

Ethology has been used in the study of human behaviour to identify
universal patterns of facial expression (Eckman, 1983), the behaviour of
premature infants (Newman, 1981) and the pain response of the newborn
(Côté, in preparation). Thus it is a particularly useful technique to
examine non-verbal behaviours, or to examine pre-verbal infants.

Frequently the behaviours are recorded on video, which is subse-
quently analyzed frame by frame, according to some preselected time
(e.g., at one minute intervals) or according to particular events that may
occur. Occasionally the data may be computerized to assist in the recognition of patterns.

The data and analysis are usually reliable, in that the video tapes may
be replayed and estimates of interrater reliability obtained. With ethology,
however, the most difficult task is that of validity, in interpreting the
meaning of the symbolic behavioural patterns.

Ethnoscience

Ethnoscience (ethnosemantics or ethnolinguistics) was developed in the
late 1960s. It evolved as social scientists attempted to increase the rigor of
ethnography which was purported to be 'soft', 'subjective', and 'non-
scientific.' Ethnoscience was viewed as a method of developing precise
and operationalized descriptions of cultural phenomena. Because the
method was viewed as more 'scientific' and because a language was
developed to describe these methods, ethnoscientists earned the label of
'logical positivists of ethnography.'

As the alternative names ethnosemantics or ethnolinguistics suggest,
ethnoscience is derived from linguistics and researchers employ the
structural analysis of phonology and grammar as a basis for data analysis.
Basically, it is a method of discovering 'how people can see their world
experience from the way they talk about it' (Frake, 1962, p. 74). The goal
of the researcher is to describe or comprehend the abstract concept,
through this analysis, from the perspective of the informants. Thus,
cultural systems are determined through the researcher's examination of
phenomenological distinctions, and those that are significant to the actors
themselves.

The underlying assumption, from structural anthropology, is that all cultural groups actively organize knowledge and rules for behaviour on the basis of culturally designated similarities and differences. To be integrated into a different cultural group, a stranger must learn the rules that are known implicitly or explictly, consciously or unconsciously, by members of that group. Each culture places certain concepts into one structure group or another. Ethnoscience, therefore, is a technique of making this implicit knowledge explicit. With implicit information, as Mead (1976) noted, the discovery of such knowledge is a mutual exploration of the topic with the informant.

Levi-Strauss (1963) summarized the process of ethnoscience in the following way. The researcher shifts from the analysis of conscious linguistic behaviour to the study of the conscious infrastructure. This process involves examining the relations between terms rather than examining the terms as independent entities. Within the cultural system the purpose of the ethnoscientist is to discover general laws, either by induction or logical deduction.

Ethnoscience interviews will differ from ethnographic interviews or questionnaires on two major dimensions. Firstly, both the questions *and* the answers are 'discovered' or elicited from the informants (Spradley and McCurdy, 1972). Secondly, the meaning of the data is significant from the informant's perspective (that is, it requires emic rather than etic analysis). With questionnaires, statistical analysis gives no interpretation to the meaning of the data, or to the organizing principles or relationships of the informant's selection of the answer.

The usefulness of ethnoscience to nursing and to the analysis of health problems has been discussed by Leininger (1969) and Evaneshko and Kay (1982). Leininger notes that through examining constructs from the nurse's perspective of health, illness or the nursing profession from the patient's perspective, gaps contributing to communication barriers between patient and professional as well as cultural discrepancies in health norms may be revealed. For example, Bush, Ullom and Osborne (1975) examined the meaning of 'mental health,' contrasting the perspective of the psychiatric mental-health professional with that of the inner-city resident. Evaneshko and Kay (1982), through their excellent description of methods, present a preliminary illustration of what *is* a medical emergency. Leininger (1969) illustrated types of health practitioner roles within a tribe in the New Guinea Highlands, while Morse (1983) examined the types of comfort and the situational factors which determined the use of each type of comfort.

The linguistic analysis used in ethnoscience is focussed on the *signification*, or the attribution of a concept and the way in which the attributes are ordered, whereas other linguistics are primarily interested in *connotation*. As an expression also connotes other images or concepts, and these connotations may not be a part of the attributes of the concept, information on the affective or behavioural data may be limited (Goodenough, 1967). The contextual material may therefore not be very rich or meaningful when ethnoscience is used alone. In *You Owe Yourself A Drunk*, Spradley (1970) added the contextual dimension by including descriptive letters from his main informant, Bill. Morse (1983), in her study of comfort, suggested that ethnoscience may be most useful to nursing when used in conjunction with other research methodologies.

As Evaneshko and Kay (1982) noted, suitable ethnoscience questions are those that answer the 'what' and ultimately, but less directly, the 'why' of cultural behaviour. Ethnoscience questions are most appropriate when the structure of a situation is the purpose of the research. For example, researchers may wish to examine, from the nurse's perspective, how they determine the attributes that identify the 'difficult' patient. From the patient's perspective the researcher may wish to determine the types of doctors, or nurses, or diseases that the patient can classify. On a broader perspective, the question might be, 'What is the structure of gift-giving in hospitals?' None of the questions arising from these problems provide affective information, that is, the questions do not ask how the patients *feel*; the only information is restricted to identifying the categories of disease, or the types, or categories, of nurses or doctors, or difficult patients.

Ethnomethodology

The purpose of ethnomethodology is to increase the understanding of taken-for-granted or implicit practices in a society. This mode of research had its origins in the sociological research of Garfinkel (1967). An ethnomethodological study usually uses documents and audio-visual taped materials that focus on everyday scenes as the source of data. The general level of research question is related to unidentified rules which govern conduct, that is, 'What taken-for-granted rules do individuals rely on and follow?' Ethnomethodologists are able to show how individuals 'unknowingly' make certain normative demands on others implicitly assuming that certain communicative competencies are possessed by others. The focus of the research is the exposure of rule use. One classic study that used this approach is Garfinkel's (1967) study of 'Agnes', a transvestite who underwent a sex-change operation. Tapes, recorded while a decision was being made regarding surgery, identified some of the taken-for-granted rules that govern a woman's behaviour. Such actions as holding a handbag, or the way a question is answered are governed by unidentified cultural norms. No studies have been identified in which nurses or nursing have been examined using this approach. One could use this approach to answer the question, 'What are the informal rules that govern a person's behaviour when he/she accepts the patient role?' Here, studying the non-compliant individual may determine the rules which are being broken. Ethnomethodology frequently focuses on the negative instance in an effort to identify the taken-for-granted rule, that is, the obverse of ethnography where the focus is on the common event.

Analytic Sociology
Analytic sociology is an offshoot of ethnomethodology engaged in by researchers who accuse ethnomethodologists of having a positivist bias (McHugh, Raffel, Foss and Blum, 1974). Analytic sociologists try to get at the deep structures of life forms through the analysis of everyday speech. The analysis focusses on the cultural or sociological applications underlying the concept of the core or basic knowledge of a society. This approach has not been widely used and may have somewhat restricted application for nursing research.

Phenomenology
Phenomenology is that kind of thinking which guides one back from theoretical abstraction to the reality of lived experience. A phenomenologist asks the question, 'What is it like to have a certain experience?' (Van Manen, 1978) In examining the qualities of experience one arrives at the essence of the experience. The phenomenological concern of our daily occupations causes us to constantly raise the question, 'What is it like to be a nurse?', then to ask the question, 'What is it that makes it possible for us to think and talk about nursing in the first place?' The phenomenologist never reaches a conclusion. The research should challenge the reader to respond by saying, 'Yes, it is like this' or 'No, I do not believe it is like that'. Phenomenologists use a wide variety of resources in attempting to find the essence of meaning. They may ask informants the question, 'What is it like for you?'. They may also obtain data from reading books and poetry on the subject, watching movies or researching others' research.

Phenomenology is not just a research method but is also a philosophy and an approach (Psathas, 1978). The birth of phenomenological philosophy is frequently attributed to Edmund Husserl. The works of the existential philosophers, Heidegger, Schuler, Sartre and Merleau-Ponty have provided the foundation for the phenomenological method when the purpose is to gather information on life experience and investigate it for its grounded structures. Phenomenology began as a philosophical reaction to the move by scientists to objectify human behaviour. As scientists became able to predict and in some cases control natural phenomena, they came to believe human behaviour could be predicted in the same way. The phenomenologist movement grew from the belief that the behaviour of people could not be controlled in the same manner that natural phenomena could be controlled.

Perhaps due to the relative newness of the discipline, phenomenology consists of several different approaches. Omery (1983) compares the work of Van Kaam, Colaizzi and Giorgi and explicates the value of each approach for those interested in phenomenology. This is a useful reference for nurses wishing to use this methodology. The main points to remember are, that phenomenology is a descriptive approach to research, that the objective is identification of the essence of behaviour, that it is based on meditative thought, and that the purpose is to promote an understanding of human beings wherever they may be found (Omery, 1983).

Phenomenology accepts experience as it exists in the consciousness of the individual. Phenomenologists maintain that intuition is important in the development of knowledge although human meaning can not be inferred from sense impression alone (Bruyn, 1966, p. 278-9). Generalization is based on similar meanings rather than an exact duplication of essence. A primary requisite of phenomenology is that there are no preconceived notions, expectations or frameworks present to guide researchers as they direct and begin to analyze the data. Phenomenology also does not presuppose the existence of process, although process may be discovered as the research takes place. The goal of phenomenology is to describe accurately the experience of the phenomenon under study and not to generate theories or models nor to develop general explanation. Some examples from the literature may help to make this point.

Gagan (1983) writes of the need to develop an understanding of the phenomenon of empathy — a characteristic viewed by many authors as germane to nursing, yet one that is little understood. Phenomenology could be used to examine this phenomenon from both client and nurse perspectives, using the initial questions: 'What is empathy like for you?' and 'What is it like for you to be empathetic?'

Davis (1978, p. 194) notes that a nurse-researcher could use skills in observation and interviewing to study a given phenomenon within the symbolic lives of the people involved. An example of this is a study (Kelpin, 1984) of the experience of giving birth. Kelpin interviewed mothers in the postpartum period to determine what the birth experience had meant to them. Field (1981) noted that giving an injection remained a stress situation for some experienced nurses and explored the meaning of giving an injection for nurses. A conflict between the need to inflict hurt and the nurse's desire to 'care for' the individual was found. Studies such as these help nurses to develop an understanding of behaviour that goes beyond the physical acts of providing care.

Some studies which are titled 'Phenomenology' would appear to be more appropriately classified as ethnography or ethnoscience, Soares' (1978) study, cited earlier, being one example of this.

SELECTING A METHOD

Given, then, that the problem is best studied by using a qualitative approach, how does a researcher select the 'best' or the most appropriate method? Again, it depends upon what one wishes to know, what the expected outcomes of the research will be, the constraints of the setting, the subjects, and, to a lesser extent, on the resources available to the researcher.

For instance, if the purpose of the research is to describe a setting or a community, then ethnography (i.e., interviews combined with participant observation) would be appropriate. But if the purpose is to describe the types of health care professionals in the community, then the question becomes more suited to an ethnoscience approach. Phenomenology would answer experiential questions such as 'What does it feel like to be a patient?' Finally, participant observation alone may be used to examine the behaviours of the people in the community as they 'become patients' in the waiting room of the hospital. For each question, there is a best or most appropriate method, and selecting the method is the most important decision in the research process.

REFERENCES

Aamodt, A.M. (1982) 'Examining Ethnography for Nurse Researchers', *Western Journal of Nursing Research*, 4(2), 209-21.

Antle-May, K. (1980) 'A Typology of Detachment and Involvement Styles Adopted During Pregnancy by First-Time Expectant Fathers', *Western Journal of Nursing Research*, 2 (2), 445-53.

Bruyn, S.R. (1966) *The Human Perspective in Sociology*, Prentice-Hall, Englewood Cliffs, New Jersey.

Bush, M.T., Ullom, J.A. and Osborne, O. (1975) 'The Meaning of Mental Health: A Report of Two Ethnoscientific Studies'. *Nursing Research*, 24(2), 130-44

Côté, J. (in preparation) A Description of the Post Operative Responses of Newborns, (on-going project), The University of Alberta, Edmonton, Alberta.

Davis, A.J. (1978) 'The Phenomenological Approach in Nursing Research' in N.L. Chaska, (ed.), *The Nursing Profession: Views Through the Mist*, McGraw-Hill, New York, pp. 186-96.

Eckman, P. (ed.) (1983) *Emotion in the Human Face*, 2nd edn. Cambridge University Press, Cambridge.

Evaneshko, V. and Kay, M.A. (1982) 'The Ethnoscience Research Technique', *Western Journal of Nursing Research*, 4(1), 49-64.

Fagerhaugh, S. and Strauss, A.L. (1977) *Politics of Pain Management*, Addison-Wesley, Menlo Park, California.

Field, P.A. (1981) 'A Phenomenological Look at Giving an Injection', *Journal of Advanced Nursing*, 6(7), 291-6.

Field, P.A. (1983) 'An Ethnography: Four Public Health Nurses' Perspectives of Nursing', *Journal of Advanced Nursing*, 8(1), 3-12.

Frake, C.O. (1962) 'The Ethnographic Study of Cognitive Systems' in T. Gladwin and W.C. Sturveant (eds.), *Anthropology and Human Behavior*, Anthropological Society of Washington, Washington, D.C., pp. 72-85.

Gagan, J.M. (1983) 'Methodological Notes on Empathy', *Advances in Nursing Science*, 5(2), 65-72.

Garfinkel, H. (1967) *Studies in Ethnomethodology*, Prentice-Hall, Englewood Cliffs, New Jersey.

Geertz, C. (1973) *The Interpretation of Cultures*, Basic Books Inc., New York.

Glaser, B.G. and Strauss, A.C. (1967) *The Discovery of Grounded Theory: Strategies for Qualitative Research*, Aldine Publishing Company, New York.

Goodenough, W.H. (1967) 'Componential Analysis', *Science*, 156, 1203-09.

Gould, J.L. (1982) *Ethology*, W.W. Norton and Company, London.

Kelpin, V. (1984) 'Birthing Pain', *Phenomenology + Pedagogy*, 2(2), 178-90.

Leininger, M. (1969) 'Ethnoscience: A Promising Research Approach to Improve Nursing Practice', *Image: The Journal of Nursing Scholarship*, 3(1), 2-8.

Levi-Strauss, C. (1963) *Structural Anthropology*, Basic Books Inc., New York.

Manis, J.G. and Meltzer, B.N. (1978) *Symbolic Interaction*, Allyn and Bacon, Boston.

McHugh, P., Raffel, S., Foss, D.C., and Blum, A.F. (1974) *The Beginning of Social Inquiry*, Routledge and Kegan Paul, London.

Mead, M. (1976) 'Toward A Human Science', *Science*, 191, 903-09.

Melia, K. (1982) '"Tell It As It Is" - Qualitative Methodology and Nursing Research: Understanding the Nurse's World', *Journal of Advanced Nursing*, 7(4), 327-36.

Morse, J.M. (1983) 'An Ethnoscientific Analysis of Comfort: A Preliminary Investigation', *Nursing Papers*, 15(1), 6-19.

Newman, L.F. (1981) 'Anthropology and Ethology in the Special Care Nursery: Communicative Functions in Low Birthweight Infants', paper presented to the Society for Applied Anthropology, Edinburgh, Scotland, April 13, 1981.

Omery, A. (1983) 'Phenomenology: A Method for Nursing Research', *Advances in Nursing Science*, 5(2), 49-63.

Psathas, C. (1978) *Phenomenological Sociology: Issues and Applications*, Wiley and Sons, New York.

Quint, J.Q. (1967) *The Nurse and the Dying Patient*, The MacMillan Company, New York.

Ragucci, A. (1972) 'The Ethnographic Approach to Nursing Research', *Nursing Research*, 21, 485-90.

Soares, C.A. (1978) 'Low Verbal Usage and Status Maintenance Among Intensive Care Nurses' in N.L. Chaska (Ed.), *The Nursing Profession: Views Through the Mist*, McGraw-Hill., New York, pp. 198-204.

Spradley, J.P. and McCurdy, D. (1972) *The Cultural Experience: Ethnography in Complex Society*, Science Research Associates, Chicago.

Spradley, J.P. (1970) *You Owe Yourself A Drunk: An Ethnography of Urban Nomads*, Little, Brown and Company, Boston.

Stern, P.N. (1978) 'Stepfather Families: Integration Around Child Discipline', *Issues in Mental Health Nursing*, 1(2), 50-6.

Tomovic, V.A. (1979) *Definitions in Sociology*, Diliton Publications, St. Catharines, Ontario.

Van Manen, M. (1978) 'Objective Inquiry into Structures of Subjectivity', *Journal of Curriculum Theorizing*, 1(1), 44-64.

Chapter Three

THE QUALITATIVE RESEARCH PROPOSAL

Preparing a qualitative research proposal to fulfill research requirements (which have generally been set out for quantitative studies) or to seek external research funding is often to find oneself in a paradoxical situation. Whereas quantitative research proposals are generally highly structured and serve as a guide to the research process, this may not be the case in qualitative research. When the quantitative proposal is developed by a student the advisory committee uses the proposal to evaluate whether or not the student is ready for data collection and has developed sound procedures with which to analyze the findings. When the proposal is to be submitted to a funding agency the researcher must convince the granting agency that funding the research is 'a good risk.'

On the other hand formulating a rigid format for research protocol, data collection and analysis is problematic when writing qualitative proposals. Qualitative researchers are frequently not in a position to describe the sample, the specific questions and the data collection procedures, as they may be unsure what the setting will eventually be like, or how many subjects will be involved. It is difficult to describe data collection and variables when the researcher is not even sure what is there in the setting. Finally, the significance of the research findings will be hard to justify until a certain level of analysis is reached. The problems of qualitative research proposals are compounded by the value placed by research committees on 'rigor' and on 'tight' research design. The philosophy of logical positivism and the relevant scientific method have been used with effectiveness in the hard sciences (such as physics and chemistry) for the past 50 years. However, these sciences work in areas where the identification of 'laws' is possible (chemical reactions are consistent when controlled). In the social sciences such control is not possible and frequently not ethical. Psychologists, when studying *behaviour*, have found that application of experimental design is limited because there are always some problems which cannot be addressed using quantitative methods. In nursing this is true to an even greater extent because we know very little about the affective aspects of illness, of being a patient, or other concerns of nursing. Until this knowledge is obtained we must continue with descriptive, rather than explanatory or predictive research. This chapter will be used to describe, step by step, one process of preparing to do research and the components of a qualitative research proposal.

STEP ONE: PREPARING TO DO RESEARCH

The very first step in preparing to do research is to decide on the research topic and to define the research problem. As stated in Chapter Two, qualitative research is used for special types of problems, the most common use being when little is known about the topic. Other characteristics such as the purpose of the research or the nature of the research question are also important. For example, it is appropriate to use qualitative methods when, in Dier's (1979) terms, you are needing to ask: 'What is going on here?', 'How do these people feel when ....?' and 'What is important when....?' (p. 54) On the other hand, it is not appropriate to use qualitative methods if all the variables are identified, and the researcher is asking, 'How many people feel this way?' or 'What is the relationship between ... and ...?' Quantitative methods are more appropriately used to measure the distribution of a phenomenon, such as attitudes, or to confirm relationships between variables.

When first discussing one's research questions with others it is easy to become discouraged. Downs (1982) in an editorial spoke of the common feedback to new investigators: 'It's a great idea, but it won't work.' Downs urges young investigators not to be discouraged by the present trend in nursing towards research which is conducted merely for the sake of doing research; one should not begin research projects simply because the variables are easy to measure. Downs notes that common discouragements to researchers at this stage may be such things as the difficulty in getting a sample, the difficulty of obtaining an appropriately qualified supervisory committee, physicians' approval, cost factors, the investigation not fitting into ongoing projects, the investigator's lack of experience and finally, the length of time taken to conduct research. If the researcher has carefully thought out the problem and recognized the need for such research, then these objections should not be the basis for discouragement.

STEP TWO: EXAMINING THE LITERATURE

There are some differences of opinion amongst qualitative researchers about the extent to which the literature should be used to guide qualitative research. There are three main viewpoints on this issue. The first view, recommended in grounded theory by Glaser (1978, p. 31), is that the researcher does not consult the literature prior to conducting fieldwork. The main argument for this position is that the literature may mislead or distract the researcher's perception and the ability to make accurate decisions in the setting. These researchers, therefore, attempt to enter the setting. The obvious disadvantage of this approach is that an extraordinary amount of time is spent 'reinventing the wheel' or rediscovering previous research. According to the second point of view, one should locate, read and utilize all information available on the research topic. Frequently this is not an extensive body of literature; therefore, this may not be an immense task. The important point is that all the major literature is incorporated into the literature review portion of the proposal, and the investigator uses this work as a plan to conduct observations in the setting or as an outline for interviews. However, the researcher risks invalidity using this method. Previous research may be based on false or biased assumptions distorting the present project, or the setting may have changed over time so that the reality has altered since the previous research was conducted.

The third method, recommended by the present authors, is to critically examine previous research and to selectively use this work. This involves obtaining all relevant literature and conducting an extensive content analysis, examining all the literature for explicit and implicit assumptions, for biases in measurement and unsubstantiated conclusions. Finally, as all settings are not the same and changes may occur over time, this literature may be used to *guide* the researcher into assisting with deriving explanations from previous research results or prevailing theories. By using this method the researchers are open and informed, but do not restrict their ability to analyze the setting by trying to fit reality into previous analyses of the situation.

STEP THREE: WRITING A FUNDING PROPOSAL

When writing a funding proposal two pitfalls may be anticipated and therefore avoided. First of all, the granting agency review committees may not understand qualitative methods and because of the rigidity and prescriptiveness of quantitative methods, reject the proposal on the basis of 'methodological flaws.' These reviewers may be concerned about the biases in the conduct and analysis of open-ended interviews, the small size of the sample and non-random methods of sample selection. Thus it is the responsibility of the applicant to explain and justify methodology.

Secondly, the review committee may be concerned at the lack of a conceptual framework to guide the research and the descriptive (rather than explanatory) nature of the research question. It is therefore necessary for the researcher to present the 'case' for the review board so that by the time the committee has read the literature review, they will understand the gaps and biases in previous research and really *want to know* the answer to the research question.

Figure 3.1 Example of a Cover Page

TITLE   OF   PROJECT

Principal Investigator
Jane C. Doe, R.N.
(Institution or agency)

Research Supervisor
L.A. Brown, SRN, PhD
(Institution or Agency)

Grant Officer
John J. Smith
Address

Before beginning to write, it is essential to identify the funding agency to which the grant will be submitted. Obtain a copy of the guidelines so that the proposal may be written to meet the agency objectives and meet requirements regarding length, format, budgetary restrictions and other specified requirements. Most importantly, the finished proposal should be completed several weeks prior to the funding agency's deadline so that the proposal may be approved by ethics committees and permission to enter research settings may be obtained. Because requirements differ, the following description of the contents of a grant proposal is presented as an example only.

Cover Page

The research proposal may be regarded as a promissory note between the researcher and the funding agency. That is, there is an 'agreement' that, if the research is funded by the agency, the researcher will conduct the project as outlined in the proposal. If, after the grant is awarded, changes in the research design are required, these must be negotiated with the granting agency. Thus most grant application guidelines contain a series of forms that contain a space for the signatures of the principal investigator and the funding officer.

However, many agencies that give small research grants may not have these forms. In this case, the researcher should add a cover page. This page contains the title of the research project, and spaces for the signatures of the principal investigator, employer, or, if the researcher is a student, the student's supervisor and the financial officer. An example is shown in Figure 3.1.

The Abstract

The abstract is a concise summary of the proposal, yet it must be comprehensive enough for the review committee to become knowledgeable about the project after reading it. As Fuller (1983) noted, the abstract usually begins with a general statement of the problem, and then summarizes the importance of the problem and method to be used. The plan for data analysis methods must be briefly described. Projected date for completion of the project and budget should also be included. The length of the abstract will be dictated by the review board. The length required may be in some cases only one hundred words, up to five hundred words. The example below fits into the latter category.

Example of an Abstract:

Title: Postpartum Sleep Patterns of Mother-Infant Dyads and the Influence of Sleep Patterns on Mother-Infant Interaction

Much has been written about the importance of mother-infant interaction during the first four weeks of the postpartum period, yet the literature is sparse in relation to information about mother-infant sleep patterns and the influence they may have in enhancing the mother-infant relationship. There is some evidence that recovery from the physiological and psychological stressors of childbirth are affected by the mother's sleep pattern. Although mother-infant sleep patterns do not synchronize, mothers make adjustments in their previous sleep needs in order to care for their infants if inadequate, 'sleep hunger' occurs and this state may be detrimental to the maternal child interaction. All changes in lifestyle are energy consuming even for individuals who are healthy and well-rested. Following delivery a mother must undergo physical restoration and establish lactation. Both processes can produce fatigue. New mothers must find the energy to care for a new infant when they may be exhausted due to physiological changes and lack of sleep. The focus of this research will be on mother-infant sleep patterns in the first four weeks of the postpartum period, and the effect that changes in the sleep patterns of both the mother and the infant have on the mother's ability to adjust to her new role, which requires that she care for and interact with her infant.

Participants will consist of a convenience sample of ten primiparous women who have given birth to live full-term infants. Data will be collected through unstructured non-directive interviews during the second, third and fourth weeks of the postpartum period. The Nursing Child Assessment Sleep Activity Record (NCASAR) and the Nursing Child Assessment Feeding Scale (NCAFS) will be used to collect information on mother-infant sleep patterns and mother-infant interaction during a feeding episode. The data from the interviews will be analyzed using the constant comparative method to generate categories. Data from the NCASAR tool will be used to verify the subject's description of their sleep patterns. Interaction scores will be calculated for each mother-infant dyad. Comparison will be made across the mother-infant pairs to establish if differences exist. If differences are established the NCAFS scores will be compared with the NCASAR scores to determine whether there is a correlation between low scores and mother-infant interaction during a feeding episode.

Information obtained from this research will provide nurses with knowledge of the factors which influence mother-infant sleep patterns during the first four weeks of the postpartum period.

Information on changes in sleep patterns, and how mothers adapt to these changes will be of use in designing nursing care to assist new mothers in preventing sleep hunger or deprivation which may influence the quality of mother-infant interaction.

(Abstract prepared by Iris Campbell, for funded proposal)

Introduction

The introduction should be a short passage explaining the problem and justifying the need for the study. These paragraphs end with a formal 'Statement of the Problem.' Under a subheading 'Delimitations of the Study' the anticipated limitations of the projected research project should be listed. To orientate the reader all terms to be used in the study are listed in alphabetical order and defined in a section 'Definition of Terms.'

Literature Review

As stated previously this section must be written to convince the reviewer that the study is worthwhile. Previous research is critiqued and the researcher demonstrates how the present project will compensate for shortcomings in previous research and will add to present knowledge. The argument is constructed in the same way in which a lawyer presents his case. The section finishes with the research question.

The literature review should also contain a short section in which the 'Implications for Nursing' are discussed. This enables the reviewer to evaluate the need for the research and the utility of the study for the nursing profession. This is particularly important when the contribution to knowledge is perhaps obscure. For example, Morse plans to examine gift-giving in hospitals. While this topic may appear obscure to a review committee, if the argument can be presented that gift-giving can be related to understanding patient-nurse relationship as reciprocity for care, the prevention of patient passivity and nurse burnout, then the committee may understand the importance of the research. This type of theoretical argument is different from a conceptual framework, in that it provides a theoretical context for the research question, but does not provide guidance for the research design. The theoretical background justifying the gift giving is not meant to identify the variables, nor the relationship between variables, as would be the case with a theoretical framework for a qualitative study.

Methodology

The methodology section should start with a short description of the setting in which the research will be conducted. The researcher should state explicitly how the research participants will be selected and any anticipated problems in obtaining a sample.

Procedures used in the research must be explained in detail. Agar (1980) notes that it is inadequate to simply write that data will be collected using 'participant observation, fieldnotes and diary'. A description with the justification and relevance for its use of each technique must be presented. Remember, it will be necessary to provide enough description to enable the reviewers to understand how data will be collected and analyzed.

The ethical constraints of the project must be listed, including plans for the storage of data, the protection of anonymity of the participants and the institution. Finally, the procedures used for data analysis and theory development must be clearly described.

Appendices

Appendix I. The first appendix is usually an anticipated schedule of work, or a time-line. This list should include a schedule of all activities from the project start date (that is, the day that funding is received) until the final report is completed. Activities for other personnel (such as research assistants, and so forth) should also be included. When calculating projected time lines, that is, time estimation for data collection, analysis and preparation of the report, allow a generous margin. It is better to complete a project early than to keep requesting additional funds and keep an agency waiting for a final report. An example of a time line is shown on Figure 3.2.

Appendix II. The second appendix contains the budget which is usually divided into sections: 'personnel', 'equipment', 'supplies' and 'other.' In the personnel section, list all persons employed on the project, including consultants who have offered to volunteer their time (listed as *gratis*), their qualifications, the total length of time and the number of hours each week they will be involved in the project.

When calculating salaries anticipate the salaries from the project *start* date. This may mean calculating salaries 10% above present levels to allow for cost of living increments that may occur in the next financial year, or from when funding is anticipated. Also include salary benefits according to the rates paid by the institution.

Requests for equipment *must match* the methodology. For example, if the method states that tape-recorded interviews will be conducted then the inclusion of a tape recorder is justified in the equipment section. Specific details of equipment required must be given, including the model number and the price. Check to ensure that requests are within the granting institution's guidelines. 'Supplies' include such items as stationery,

TIME LINE

D U R A T I O N (months)

ACTIVITY	Jan	Feb	Mar	Apr	May	Jun	Jul	Aug	Sep	Oct	Nov	Dec
Preparation of Proposal												
Gaining Approval/Entry												
Data Collection												
Data Analysis												
Preparation of the Final Report												

Figure 3.2 Example of a Time-Line

audio tapes and telephone calls. If the project is to continue beyond one year, do not forget to add an increase of budget for each year of 6-10% to allow for inflation. An example of a budget is shown on Figure 3.3.

Appendix III. The next appendix contains letters of approval from the institution in which the research will be conducted. As such approval usually involves ethical and administrative clearance by the institution, investigators must allow adequate time for this review. It may take at least four weeks but frequently the review process will take longer. It is important to find out in advance how long an agency takes to provide such clearance as failure to allow enough time to obtain approval may result in missing a funding deadline.

Letters from influential persons supporting the study may assist the researcher's cause for committee review. Solicit letters from persons who are known for expertise in the area of research which is being pursued. Request that letters are written which emphasize the need for and the significance of the research.

Most agencies require that the proposal include a copy of the informed consent form to be used by the participants and often a written example of how the researcher will explain the research procedures, including the time involvement, to participants. This explanation must be written using the exact words that will be used to explain the project.

Appendix IV. Finally, attach vitae for the principal investigator and all other key personnel, so the reviewers may be assured that the researchers are qualified to conduct the research, or that they have access to consultants to assist in areas where experience or expertise may be lacking. If the researcher is a student, the vitae of the student's supervisor should also be attached.

Appendix V. The final appendix is the informed consent form. An example is shown in Figure 3.4.

INFORMED CONSENT

Basically, informed consent is obtaining the

> 'knowing consent of an individual or his legally authorized representative, so situated as to be able to exercise free power of choice without undue inducement or any element of force, fraud, deceit, duress or other forms of constraint or coercion' (Annas, Glantz and Katz, 1977, p. 291).

Usually informed consent consists of the following components:
- An explanation of the purpose of the research and the procedures to

Figure 3.3 Example of A Budget Page

Budget

Personnel

Susan J. Smith, RN, PhD Principal Investigator $3,500.00
    10% time / 12 months @ $35,000* PA
M.N. Jones, RN, MN Project Director
    50% time / 12 months @ $24,600* PA $12,300.00
I.M. Nurse, RN, BSc, Research Assistant
    100% time / 12 months $18,200* PA $18,200.00
N.O. Rutherford, Typist
    30 hrs/week / 10 months @ $10.50/hour <u>$12,600.00</u>
                        Subtotal $46,600.00

Equipment

1 Julex Portable Tape Recorder #ABC-12345 $ 89.95
    with external microphone
1 Julex Transcriber   <u>$546.00</u>
                        Subtotal $635.95

Supplies

36 Audio cassettes @ $3.49 each $125.64
Paper and sundries   <u>$200.00</u>
                        Subtotal $325.64

Other

Rental / 1 typewriter
    for 10 months @ $50.00/month $500.00
Photocopying $300.00
Printing and binding of final report   <u>$850.00</u>
                      Subtotal $1,650.00

                    TOTAL <u>$49,211.59</u>

* Salary includes 8% indirect benefits

be followed;
- A description of the risks inherent in the research and of any benefits that may be obtained from participating;
- The opportunity for the prospective participant to ask any questions regarding the research, and a statement stating that these questions have been satisfactorily answered;
- The information that the participant is free to withdraw at any time or may refuse to answer any questions without penalty.

Informed consent may be said to have been obtained when the person is knowledgeable, that is, has been informed about all procedures and no deceit or concealment has been used; has exercised *voluntary choice*, without coercion; and was competent to freely choose. In addition, the individual must not be under the legal age for consent, a part of a 'captive' population, or mentally incompetent.

These requirements for informed consent were developed in the United States in response to abuses of subjects by biomedical experimental researchers. Because of differences in the relationship between the researcher and the subject in experimental research and between the researcher and the informant or participant in fieldwork situations, Cassell (1980) has argued that this method of obtaining consent is inappropriate for anthropologists and others conducting ethnography. However, at this time, this is the only model available for obtaining consent and all ethical guidelines are written and proposals evaluated using this model.

Initially consent is obtained verbally, followed by the formal consent, that is, reading and signing of the consent form. If the participant cannot read, or if it is not convenient to obtain written consent (such as with telephone interviews), then verbal consent may be obtained. If the verbal consent can be tape recorded, then this provides a permanent record of the consent procedure for the researcher. In order to ensure anonymity and to separate the informant's name from the data, record the consent portion onto a separate tape kept solely for this purpose and erase the consent from the interview tape.

'Implied consent' is frequently used when coercion is low. For example, consent may be implied when the respondent completes a mailed questionnaire and returns it to the researcher. It may be assumed that the respondent consents to participate in the study as s/he has freely completed and returned the questionnaire. The alternative would be to put the questionnaire in the waste-paper basket.

Another example of implied consent is the confidential use of hospital records for research purposes. By consenting to admission and treatment in a research hospital the patients are giving implied consent for their

Figure 3.4 An Example of an Informed Consent Form

UNIVERSITY OF ALBERTA
FACULTY OF NURSING

Informed Consent Form

PROJECT TITLE: Becoming a Mother
INVESTIGATOR: Dr. J. Doe   Phone: 654-3210
The purpose of this research project is to increase nurses' understanding of patients' experiences when first admitted to hospital. Interviews will be conducted at least three times and each interview will last approximately one hour. During these interviews questions will be asked regarding your feelings about being a patient. These tapes will not be shared with the ward staff, but the final report, containing anonymous quotations, will be available to all at the end of the study.

There may be no direct benefits to the participants of this study, but there may be changes in patient care following the completion of this study.

THIS IS TO CERTIFY THAT I, _____

(print name)

HEREBY agree to participate as a volunteer in the above named project.

I understand that there will be no health risks to me resulting from my participation in the research.

I hereby give permission to be interviewed and for these interviews to be tape-recorded. I understand that, at the completion of the research, the tapes will be erased. I understand that the information may be published, but my name will not be associated with the research.

I understand that I am free to deny any answer to specific questions on the questionnaires. I also understand that I am free to withdraw my consent and terminate my participation at any time, without penalty.

I have been given the opportunity to ask whatever questions I desire, and all such questions have been answered to my satisfaction.

_____   _____   _____
Participant   Witness   Researcher

                                                            _____
                                                            Date

hospital records to be used for research purposes. However, such projects must be cleared through the institution's ethics committee and the researcher is expected to protect the confidentiality of the records including the patients' identities.

When wishing to conduct research on 'special populations' such as prison inmates, hospitalized patients or school children, it is necessary to obtain several levels of consent. Firstly, consent must be obtained from the institution responsible for the individuals who will be participants in the study. The administrator or the ethical review committee will examine the proposal to determine that the health of those for whom they are responsible will not be jeopardized by the proposed research.

The next level of consent must be obtained from the legal guardian of patients (if the proposed subjects are mentally incompetent or if they are children). Finally, the individuals who will participate in the research must also give their own consent to participate, even if the participant is a child. In this case, verbal consent is adequate.

There are exceptions to obtaining parental consent and such decisions will need to be made by an ethics committee. One example of this would be if the researcher wished to study adolescent pregnancy, when informing the parents of the study also meant informing them of their daughter's pregnancy, which would be a violation of the adolescent's privacy.

The Ongoing Nature of Consent

Having obtained informed consent at the beginning of the study the researcher must recognize that consent may be revoked at any time by the participant. For instance, if in the middle of an interview an informant says: 'Just between you and me...', s/he is probably withdrawing permission for the researcher to use that information in the study. If in doubt, check with informant to see if the information so obtained may be included.

Occasionally the project will start well and then the participant will change his/her mind about participating in the research. The participant may withdraw from the study and leave the researcher with an incomplete set of data, or the participant may choose to withdraw all information collected about him/her from the study. This is the participant's privilege.

Another aspect of informant consent, especially with participant observation, is the continual nature of data collection. Data collection does not stop when the tape recorder is turned off and participants tend to forget this. Frequently, when the stage of trust is reached, informants will treat the researcher as a peer and may, as one example, share secrets. This requires frequent and gentle reminders from the researcher ('Remember the study...') and permission to include that data. If permission is denied, the information cannot be included and must be discarded.

The Use of Photographs
Consent for the use and publication of photographs must also be obtained from the participant. In the case of photographs, the consent form should contain a clause in which the participant 'releases all rights to the photographs' and it is clear that the photographs and the negatives become the property of the researcher.

THE POLITICS OF RESEARCH

When preparing a proposal the political and ethical ramifications of the research must be considered. The costs of the research, both financial and psychological, to the institution and the subjects will be assessed by an ethics committee prior to giving permission for entry or for funding.

Entering an institution to conduct research is a privilege, not a right. The presence of a researcher in an institution is not without costs and risks to the host institution.

Consider, if the researcher wishes to observe and interview staff, on whose time will these interviews be conducted? Will it be on the 'agency's' time when the staff member is on duty, or on the staff member's own time, after duty? Furthermore, researchers take up space and impede work patterns. This increases the workload for other staff members and may be translated into indirect costs for the institution.

Also, the institution experiences some risks by permitting a researcher to make observations related to patient care. It is possible that the researcher may observe (and report) 'untoward, unfortunate incidents' which may result in a patient or his family suing the hospital. The researcher's observations, even though confidential, may be subpoenaed and used as evidence in court. Therefore, unless the institution is interested in the research question and can perceive some benefits resulting from the research, permission to conduct the study may not be given.

MORAL/ETHICAL CONDUCT

Fieldwork introduces special moral and ethical problems that are not usually encountered by other researchers. In becoming a part of the setting, the researcher is exposed to all aspects of the environment. Even if those aspects from which the moral and ethical dilemmas arise are not a part of the research study, the researcher, by virtue of being present, and being a witness, has a responsibility to the participants. The following example for discussion illustrates one dilemma arising from such situations:

As a part of her thesis requirements, Joan chose to examine

the supportive/therapeutic relationships among patients in a psychiatric ward. She had a great deal of difficulty getting access into the only psychiatric hospital in the city where she lived. (Actually, the process of approval took 6 1/2 months of her second year.) Finally, she was permitted to observe and to conduct interviews in a 'less sick' ward.

After two months she felt more relaxed in the setting, and the staff and the patients began to trust her. Occasionally patients reported to Joan that staff members 'hated' and 'were mean' to them. Joan recorded these statements in her fieldnotes, but as examining the staff-patient relationship was not included in her research question, she was careful to avoid such discussions during taped interviews. She noted in her fieldnotes that she thought certain patients were paranoid.

One day, however, Joan arrived on the ward to find the place in an uproar. A patient accused a staff member of 'rough-handling' her. The patient had a large bruise on her back. The staff member denied the allegations. The patients appealed to Joan for help.

This example represents a typical dilemma in a fieldwork situation. In this case the subjects of Joan's study were in a powerless position, yet they perceived Joan (also in a powerless situation) as being more powerful and filling the role of advocate. Although Joan had conducted observations in the ward for two months, she had not observed any abusive behavior of the staff towards the patients, and due to the psychiatric illnesses experienced by the patients, it is possible that the allegations were not true. On the other hand, more than one patient had reported negative attitudes of the staff towards the patients.

Joan feels she has a lot to lose by 'taking sides'. She would lose more than a year of work, including the time taken to prepare a proposal, to gain entry and to start data collection. While presenting what she had been told by the patients would add credence to their complaints, it would also result in Joan having to withdraw from the setting. As she has no alternative research setting in her town, if she withdrew she would have to travel to another town or start again with another question, another proposal.... What should Joan do?

Estroff and Churchill (1984, p. 15) note that two of the most problematic situations for the researcher in a clinical setting are: (1) 'Getting caught between the patients and staff, and (2) being privy to unethical and perhaps illegal conduct by staff.' They point out that, in the clinical setting, *both* the patients and the staff are the research subjects regardless of the focus of the research question. Refusing to become involved in such a situation in order to maintain access to the research setting is indefensible, as it places the value of the research *per se* above the quality of life of the patient.

Joan is not in a position to 'know' if all, some or one member of the staff are involved in the present situation. One thing is clear: staff-patient relationships have deteriorated to a 'non-therapeutic' level. Therefore, one of Joan's goals must be to assist in the reconstruction of staff-patient relationships without taking sides.

If Joan does have 'evidence' of staff maltreatment of patients, even if this evidence is in the form of patient reports, she is obligated to report these events to the physician-in-charge. To remain silent and do nothing involves Joan in the abuse problem. A possible way to avoid these dilemmas is to anticipate the witnessing of undesirable events and to make prior reporting arrangements clear with the staff, so that prearranged procedures may be followed should an unfortunate event occur. Having such channels identified will not prevent the conflict involved with such incidents, but it will set out an orderly, professional standard to be followed that will 'respect the rights and obligations of all interested parties' (Estroff and Churchill, 1984, p. 15).

REFERENCES

Agar, M. (1980) *The Professional Stranger: An Informal Introduction to Ethnography*, Academic Press, Inc., New York.

Annas, G.J., Glantz, L.H. and Katz, B.F. (1977) *Informed Consent to Human Experimentation: The Subject's Dilemma*, Ballinger Publishers, Cambridge, Massachusetts, p. 291.

Cassell, J. (1980) 'Ethical Principles for Conducting Fieldwork', *American Anthropologist*, 82, 28-41.

Diers, D. (1979) *Research in Nursing Practice*. J.B. Lippincott Company, Philadelphia.

Downs, F.S. (1982) 'It's a Great Idea — But It Won't Work', *Nursing Research*, 31, 4.

Estroff, S.E. and Churchill, L.R. (1984) 'Comment 1 (Ethical Dilemmas)', *Anthropology Newsletter*, 25(7), 15.

Fuller, E.O. (1983) 'Preparing an Abstract of a Nursing Study', *Nursing Research*, 32(5), 316-7.

Glaser, B. (1978) *Theoretical Sensitivity*, The Sociology Press, Mill Valley, California.

Chapter Four

PREPARING TO DO RESEARCH

Once the proposal is completed and ethical clearance obtained the researcher still has some preparation to do prior to commencing data collection. This entails gaining access to both the agency and the informants (subjects) and planning the data gathering. Planning the data gathering involves selecting appropriate equipment and becoming familiar with its use.

GAINING ENTRANCE TO A FORMAL ORGANIZATION

In order to gain access to the group to be studied the researcher must first obtain access to the formal organization. Informal contacts with members of the organization can be used to get valuable information on how to access the institution and the steps required for ethical clearance. Insight into the formal and informal structure of the hierarchy of the group may also be obtained.

It is helpful to determine whether or not an agency will consider allowing a study to be conducted before the formal proposal is written, as this prevents unnecessary expenditure of time and energy if the research is not considered feasible by the organization. For example, an organization may have too many research studies in progress in that area and perceive that they have reached the saturation point. Once the formal clearance is completed entry to the study group can proceed.

If a study is to be conducted in a hospital or public health agency the supervisor may well be the gatekeeper to the group to be studied. In an in-hospital study the physician may also be part of the gatekeeping group. The more contacts made and the more explanation given in person to the key people, the more likely it is that the study will be accepted. If the nursing supervisor is supportive it is probable that the nursing staff will be as well. As far as possible, when in the planning stage of the research project, include some of the key people from the institution. This will tend to increase their commitment to the study. Even before approaching the top hierarchy it is wise to seek out those who will be directly involved in the study. They will probably be consulted by the administration before ethical clearance to conduct the research is given. Also, if clearance is given without the potential subjects knowing what is involved they are less likely to be co-operative when the study is introduced.

As a means of entry into an organization, Field (1980) was given permission to speak to all the public health nurses employed by an agency at a general meeting. The study was submitted to the agency for approval only after it was apparent that the nurses were interested in taking part in the research. When two clinics were selected for the study further meetings were held with the staff to ensure that they were fully aware of the nature of the study.

GAINING ENTRY TO THE STUDY GROUP

When using a qualitative design, which involves the researcher as data gatherer, entry to the field is not assured once consent for the study has been given. The researcher will have to establish credibility with the sub-groups which are to be studied. There is debate in the literature as to whether or not male anthropologists can obtain accurate information on women's cultural activities in pre-industrialized society (Gregory, 1984) or whether women anthropologists can converse openly with men in American Indian cultures (Wax, 1971, p. 46) or obtain information on men's activities (Bowen, 1964; Golde, 1970). Similarly, it may be questioned whether nurse-researchers can get accurate information on the perceptions of patients if they are seen to be a part of the nursing fraternity. Patients may perceive the nurse-researcher to be one of the power group and worry about ramifications if they report negative instances of care. The way in which researchers present themselves to a group may therefore be crucial to subsequent acceptance.

In *Street Corner Society*, Whyte (1955) outlined the difficulty he had gaining an entrance to the lower-income Italian community that he studied. He made several abortive attempts until he was introduced to "Doc", the leader of a street corner group. As a friend of Doc's he was accepted by the group, but only after he was able to converse and act in a manner seen as appropriate to the group was he incorporated as a member. Kratz (1975) noted that her experience as a nurse helped her to establish her credibility with nurses. Pearsall (1965) suggested that while a nurse studying nursing has advantages in relation to background knowledge, there is nevertheless a danger of overlooking relevant data because of the familiarity of the context. Entry may be facilitated into a group but objectivity may be impeded when nurses study nursing. This is a particular jeopardy when a nurse enters a setting in which she has previously worked.

As mentioned in Chapter 3, when entering the field the informants will want to know details of the methodology and the purpose of the study. It is important not to conceal information but it is necessary to keep explanations simple, brief and to the point. It is also important to indicate the type of information that will be used in the final document. It may be necessary to tell the informants that the content will evolve as the study progresses. Establishing trust is essential as a first step in gaining entry to the group.

Another concern is whether or not the observer will disrupt the nursing care. It is sometimes useful to prepare for data collection by entering the setting and identifying ways in which data can be collected which are not intrusive to the nurse and client. For example, Kratz (1975) found that notetaking resulted in a breakdown of the relationships she had established with her nurse subjects. She decided that she would have to record notes after the interviews if she was to retain rapport with the subjects. The researcher must be sensitive and responsive to the problems of the informants. If the researcher's schedule can be fitted around the nurses' schedules the likelihood of being accepted will increase. However, it is important that the researcher achieve a balance between informants' needs and the researcher's need to be involved in observation at varying times if a representative picture of the setting is to be obtained.

A frequent problem that is voiced at the outset of a study relates to the researcher's use of findings. In order to obtain ethical clearance the purpose of the study and the mode of data presentation will have been identified. This information will also need to be shared with the informants. When there are multiple investigators, inform the subjects who will have access to the raw data and how the confidentiality of the information provided will be maintained. If early observations are treated as a feasibility study it is possible to meet again, if necessary, with the informants and renegotiate the "contract" with them.

Informants may wonder why *they* have been invited to participate in the study. The interest of nurse-researchers will probably be in studying nursing problems or care-giving with the goal of improving care. It is important therefore to inform informants of this goal and to make it clear that while they may not directly benefit from the study it is hoped that other patients will benefit in the future.

Try not to make unrealistic promises. It is not wise to share fieldnotes or give early feedback. Making informants aware of early findings may result in self-consciousness and behavioural change which could jeopardize the findings. Clarify the observer's role. Determine whether or not the researcher will become involved with nursing care and ensure this decision is communicated to all staff. In one study the observer did help provide physical care, such as positioning a child for lumbar puncture (Toohey, 1984) but did not become involved in other aspects of care. This was a point the observer had to reinforce with the nurses over the course of the study so they did not expect her to help with care when the department was busy.

In interview studies the researchers may work with individuals rather than with groups, but the same process is needed to establish trust. In the case of studies of documents, the archivists will need to assure themselves of the researchers' trustworthiness and the purpose of the study before access to documents is granted.

Negotiating admission to a setting is time consuming, it takes patience and may not always be achieved within the estimated time-frame. Gaining entry requires flexibility on the part of the researcher as informants must be seen at their convenience and data gathering techniques may have to be adjusted if access is to be secured.

Approach the gatekeeper appropriately according to the organizational norms. Some organizations are more formal than others, discussion over coffee will be appropriate in some, while in others a more formal approach is needed. Remember, small courtesies may make the difference between being accepted or rejected by the host organization. The researcher is the guest.

Establishing Rapport

It is essential that the researcher fit into the setting with minimal disruption. Attention should be paid to the institutions dress code and language and the researcher should try to abide by the group norms as nearly as possible. While it is important to establish commonalities with the group, at the same time there is a need to keep a low profile. While the researcher must establish credibility, to try to be better than the group will not be helpful in gaining their acceptance.

Developing Relationships

While it is important to be accepted as part of the group, the researcher must avoid becoming too friendly with individual members. If friendships develop there is a risk that the researcher and informant will lose sight of the purpose of the research. Confidences may be exchanged that can unwittingly become unethical in terms of the research and this is how the researcher can lose objectivy and become caught in a bind of conflicting loyalties and interests.

FIRST DAYS IN THE FIELD

Establishing Trust

For even the most experienced observer the first days in the field are difficult. The researcher does not know the behaviours that are expected and is afraid of making mistakes. Even walking into the organization to be studied is frightening. Once inside the tension eases, and the first hurdle is overcome.

The first contact is hard because the researcher is an outsider, a stranger to the group. The researcher must be able to accept the laughter of others when a mistake in etiquette is made and be alert to behaviours that to the researcher are suitable but which may be regarded as insulting to the group. As noted by Wax (1971):

> The person who cannot abide feeling awkward or out of place, who feels crushed whenever he makes a mistake — embarrassing or otherwise — who is psychologically unable to endure being, and being treated like, a fool, not only for a day or a week but for months on end, ought to think twice before he decides to become a participant observer. (p. 370)

Once the researcher becomes familiar with the norms and values in the setting things *will* improve. An individual who can not live with ambiguity will not be suited to field research (Wax, 1971, p. 370).

It may be useful to spend a week in the study area prior to the commencement of formal data gathering. This period can be used to get the participants acclimatized to the researcher's observations and use of tape recorders or video cameras in the setting. During this period the researcher should engage in all activities planned for the data gathering period. The researcher must become familiar with the conversational patterns and normal behaviour of the informants during this period. The organization of the group and the social interaction patterns within the group, as well as the informal leaders, should be identified. This period is critical as the observer seeks acceptance from the participants and establishes the research role.

There are some steps that can be taken to reduce the initial awkwardness of entering a group. The first step is to have an insider, that is, a group member, introduce the researcher personally to the group. Do not expect the first weeks to be productive. The initial period is used to get to know the participants while at the same time they are getting to know the researcher. Consider this phase as the time in which the feasibility of the study is tested. Then, because it has already been acknowledged that this is a trial or practice period, mistakes are less embarrassing.

Wax (1971) notes that when entering a group it is important to initially align oneself with those working in the lowest positions in the hierarchy. When entering a ward setting this means first gaining the trust of the nurse aides and the orderlies, then the student nurses, the staff nurses, and, finally, the charge nurse or ward sisters. It is not possible to reverse this order and still be successful in gaining the trust of the whole group. People of lower status are suspicious of those who are 'close' to those who have power over them, and will be concerned that the researcher is providing the superiors with information.

It is useful to restrict one's enquiry to asking general questions in the first few days. Avoid topics that seem to cause discomfort or controversy to the informants. Above all, listen, learn the language and the values of the group. It is difficult to remember what everyone is saying when first entering a group. Do not try, otherwise panic will result. Rather, try to get a feeling for what is happening and use the time to become accustomed to the setting.

As people are introduced show interest in them. Establish eye contact that helps in developing trust. A smile covers nervousness and may help put informants at ease. It is important to answer questions as directly as possible. If asked to attend social events with the group it is important to accept the invitation as it is another indication that they are also accepting you.

During these first days in the field observe the organizational and power structure. Make notes on the setting and organization at this stage. Who are the formal leaders? Who are the informal leaders? Who are likely to be key informants? For example, the researcher may be studying nurses but the unit clerk may provide critical insights which would not be gathered from the nurses themselves. During this period in the field act like a sponge, absorb all the information possible. When some grasp of the information is reached then start to filter the data that has been absorbed. Make notes on everything, even if it does not appear useful and relevant at the time. In this way a more accurate picture of the context for the research will be obtained. Failure to record the obvious may lead to it being ignored or omitted, a problem to which the researcher must always be alert when undertaking qualitative studies.

Finding Space

When a researcher enters the area where the study is to be conducted, it is necessary to find a space in which to work, in order to complete fieldnotes or diary entries throughout the day. Therefore, when negotiating entry also negotiate space for writing and interviewing. In ideal situations the researcher may be provided with an office with a desk and even with a locked file, but it is more likely that the space will be a cramped corner in a storage room. The key factor is that the researcher needs space to write, undisturbed, so that fieldnotes can be completed reasonably close to an event's occurrence.

If there is no chance for the researcher to have a private assigned space it will be necessary to negotiate shared space or find an unused corner in which to withdraw. A space that the researcher can use is essential if accuracy of data is to be maintained.

SELECTING KEY INFORMANTS

Depending on the research question, informants may be obtained either from the community or from informal or formal group settings. If, for example, the researcher is examining breastfeeding practices, mothers who are nursing infants may be solicited from the community by requesting referrals from community health clinics or by using advertising methods to request volunteers. Even though some of these informants have volunteered to participate in the study, some will be more receptive to the interviewer and more articulate than others, and, therefore, be better informants. The researcher may not use all informants equally.

If the research is to be conducted in an organization or with an informal group, there are key people who have more insight into the norms and values of the institution than others. It is important to identify these people and to obtain information from them. The researcher must be careful, however, not to ignore quiet, less verbally expressive individuals as they may have a different perspective on the institution. It is often easier to start data gathering with the more extroverted informant.

Douglas (1976, p. 213-5) observed that any setting has at least four types of people that may be useful to the ethnographer. The first he labels 'social gadflies.' These are well-liked, lively but low-key people. They have the ability to mix and to talk to almost anyone in the group. The second type are the 'constant observers, or everyday life historians.' These people are frequently older, long-established members of the group, who enjoy recalling details from past events. Next, the 'everyday life philosophers' are people who think a great deal about a setting, can provide insights into what is going on, but are generally less vocal than the 'constant observers.' Finally, 'marginal people' are people who do not really belong in the group or who feel ambivalent about the group and are the most common type of person used as an informant. Because of their split loyalties they are able to describe an inside view and they are also often willing to divulge information to an outsider. However, as they are often not completely trusted by the group, aligning oneself with 'marginal people' may stigmatize the researcher and impede the development of trust with other group members.

An informant may be any person who is willing to talk to the researcher. Informants are the key to sound ethnographic research and may supply the majority of the information needed, or complement data provided through observation, interviews, chart analysis or other techniques. An informant is willing to answer questions and to provide information in an informal give-and-take situation. When talking with informants the aim of the researcher is to find the things that are important to them and their understanding of the subject being researched. Because a researcher cannot be in all places at all times, the informant helps fill in gaps in the data and act as a culture broker explaining the cultural rules, values and norms within that setting.

Nevertheless the informant may know only a part of the total social situation. Thus the acquisition of several informants, who represent different sectors of the group is important. The use of several informants also helps to verify information. In a study of nursing, for example, the view of the supervisor, the graduate nurse, the patient, the physician and the ancilliary workers, may all be needed to understand the complex culture of a hospital ward. Germain (1979) illustrates this complexity in her study of a cancer ward. To understand the nurses behaviour it was necessary to understand the norms and values of the total system.

In a busy organization, important conversations may take place over coffee or lunch or, in the community health setting, in the car driving from one appointment to the next. The researcher must take advantage of all such opportunities but it should be made clear to informants that information obtained in these situations will be included in the study.

Once a relationship with a key informant has been established, the data acquisition will frequently snowball. The first informant will often introduce the researcher to other informed persons in the organization. The researcher should be careful, however, not to restrict informants only to those persons acquired in this way, otherwise the information obtained may be biased.

However, it is not usually possible to do in-depth interviews on all members in a setting. As stated previously, key informants are selected according to their role and knowledge or insights into the setting, and the type of relationship they have with others in the setting. Another criterion for selection is the amount of rapport and trust potential informants have developed with the researcher and their willingness to participate in the research. If a key informant is not receptive to the researcher or to the project, then interviews with that person will be shallow and perhaps invalid as the informant will not disclose true feelings and may give only partial information on the topic. If the researcher does not have any choice and considers it essential to interview that person, then it is advisable for the researcher to take time and wait until a relationship develops before interviewing that person.

Thus it is important to note that the process of selecting informants in qualitative research is not done randomly. Selecting informants by statistical chance may severely affect the quality of the data because the informant selected by chance may not be co-operative nor be the best informed on the topic. However, by using such a subjective method to select informants to interview, it becomes important to constantly verify information obtained with secondary informants. Depending on the research topic, secondary informants may be all other persons within the same setting, or people in similar situations in other settings. In the first case, interviews with secondary informants may be more structured but still open-ended, so that the questions do not 'lead' the informant. In the second case, where the key informants are anonymous, the researcher may be more direct in verifying data or confirming the researcher's hunches. For example, when studying weaning practices, the researcher may approach other mothers who are weaning and ask: 'Some mothers have told me that weaning a toddler is just a matter of discipline. What do you think?'

These techniques of 'sampling' in ethnographic research have been criticized by quantitative researchers as the non-random nature of subject selection limits generalizability. Remember, the purpose of qualitative research is to discover *meaning*, not to measure the distribution of attributes within a population (Morse, 1984). Thus, the question of generalizability is not necessarily pertinent to factor-identifying research.

GATHERING DATA

For many researchers one of the difficulties in beginning data collection is a lack of familiarity with the equipment needed in the field. With increasing technology audio or visual recording is frequently being used as a means of increasing validity of the data. The most commonly used pieces of equipment are tape-recorders, 35mm cameras and video cameras. While many people now own and operate such equipment at home, it is critical that the researcher is familiar with their operation and is able to obtain good quality pictures or recordings before commencing data collection.

Once the equipment has been mastered it is still critical to test it out in the data gathering situation. Placement of equipment may be dictated by space, for example, furniture may have to be rearranged to allow room for a video camera. A child banging blocks in the playroom may obscure a recording in an adjacent interview room. A flash camera may change the informant's behavior and it may be necessary to use a faster film rather than use the flash. When using a video camera it will also be necessary to experiment to find how to get the best angle without moving the camera. These are things that can only be determined through trial and error during the initial days in the field.

Some practical advice on equipment will be presented, but with the many brands available these guidelines will be general. Each researcher must take the advice and apply it to the guidelines provided by the manufacturers of the equipment to be used in a particular study.

Tape Recorders

Generally a cassette recorder is used for data gathering. Cassette tapes come in a variety of lengths: 45 minutes, 60 minutes and 90 minutes recording time are the commonest that are available. Half the time is on each side of the tape. Recently some double space tape has become available that allows twice the recording space. At the present time the cost of this tape probably outweighs the benefits. It is advisable to select a tape size that goes beyond the expected length of the interview as constantly changing the tape will affect the quality of the interview and make the informant more conscious of the recording.

Select a good quality tape recorder, one with a conference pick-up range of six feet from the source of the conversation, or one that takes a lapel microphone, as this will be less likely to disturb the informant. The use of an extension microphone attached to the cassette recorder allows the interviewer more mobility during the interview process. Check on the quality of sound at the beginning of each interview; poor sound makes transcription either difficult or impossible and data will be lost. It also takes more time to transcribe and therefore is more expensive in relation to secretarial services.

Place the cassette recorder as unobtrusively as possible so that it will not distract the informant's attention. Always carry an extension cord, adaptors and fresh batteries. In North America old houses do not always have three-pin plugs and this can result in lost data if one arrives unprepared.

A recorder that signals the end of a side on the tape is helpful as the researcher then knows when to turn the cassette. If the recorder does not have a signal, a timer can be used, although it is still critical to watch carefully to see when the tape ends. Interviewing beyond the end of the tape may represent a considerable amount of lost data.

Other characteristics that are useful when selecting a tape-recorder are the presence of a counter and the ability of the recorder to be set at different speeds. A counter enables the researcher to locate a particular incident on the tape with relative ease. Variable speed allows the tape to be played through quickly, permitting the researcher to hear the voices, without change in tone, despite the increased speed. It can also be played slowly if a particular passage is difficult to comprehend at normal speed.

There is a danger in using batteries in that they may run out, or if their potency is low the quality of the recording may be poor. It is useful to carry batteries in case a recording may need to be made where an electrical source is not available. An example of this would be interviewing public health nurses in their cars following home visits.

Telephone jacks are another essential piece of equipment that may be used with a tape recorder. These consist of a microphone built into a suction cup. This cup adheres to the telephone receiver and, when the jack is plugged into the connector labelled 'mic', provides a recording of both parties conversing on the telephone.

Thirty-Five Millimeter Cameras

While most people know how to use a camera it is critical to obtain the correct exposure and a clear picture if part of the data base is to be photographs. When engaged in research do not economize by buying a cheap camera and hoping it will do the job. For the inexperienced photographer a modern 35mm camera, with a built-in light meter and focal plane shutter, is probably the best buy. The camera should be a single-lens reflex, with interchangeable lenses.

For indoor photography it is best to mount the camera on a tripod. If the shutter speed is less than 1/50 of a second a hand-held camera will probably result in a fuzzy picture, which is generally not acceptable for research purposes.

If the researcher wishes to focus on facial expression a telephoto lens will probably be essential. However, if the researcher's interest is in movement, e.g. posture for lifting, a normal lens will probably be suitable. If the purpose of the research is to obtain a pictorial record of the setting, for example, a birthing room, a wide-angle lens will provide the best detail. Inexperienced photographers should find an expert photographer, describe the project and ask advice on the best equipment and the speed of film that is likely to produce the best results for the research.

For publication purposes, black and white film is preferable but colour slides are necessary for classrooms or conference presentation. It is advisable to take photographs in both mediums. For indoor settings a fast film is required. To reiterate, consents must be obtained from each recognizable person in a photograph before they can be used for research or publication.

Videotape Recording (VTR)

Videotape recording is used most commonly in stimulated recall and ethology as a mode of data collection. When the data base is a videotape it is critical that the equipment is in first-class working order and that new tapes are used. Breakdowns cause delays and loss of valuable data.

For research purposes a half-inch reel-to-reel tape is preferable to cassettes as it permits instant stops at specific points. The three-quarter-inch cassettes do not have this degree of flexibility. Tapes can also be time-marked if the timing of the event is an element of analysis.

It is preferable to use the same set of equipment throughout a research project as machines tend to have their own idiosyncracies. This increases the user's confidence in the equipment and also avoids unsettling the participants with the introduction of equipment that might be noticeably different.

All equipment should be set up ahead of filming and should be checked to see that sound and film images are clear. One researcher (Conners, 1978) recommended that the lens opening ring be set at f/2 for indoor filming as a smaller aperture left the image too dark. When focussing the camera it is preferable to set the focus ring at infinity and then zoom in on an object to cover the smallest point required. The focus ring should then be adjusted to obtain a clear image. Avoid focussing on windows when setting the camera, otherwise the image will be too dark when the camera is focussed on the subject.

The placement and the taping of extension cords to the floor are important considerations if the camera is being used in a patient care area. They must not be hazardous to patients' safety. Check the regulations in the institution where the research is being conducted. Electrical equipment used in patient areas may have to be approved by the engineering department.

It is important to monitor the film quality throughout a recording session. This can be done by checking the image in the camera or the image on the TV screen. The sound can be checked by using an earplug, and this approach does not disturb the participants. Checking the sound is important if there is movement in the room which might cause the microphone to become disconnected.

Other points to check include setting the VTR counter at zero and checking that the record button is depressed on the VTR machine. A directional microphone is usually adequate to pick up general questions and answers in a group setting. The microphone selected should be tested prior to the official data collection period.

Summary

In conclusion, gaining entry to an organization requires both patience on the part of the researcher and sensitivity to the interactions that are occurring between the researcher and potential informants in the host agency. Any equipment that is to be used should be checked and the researcher should be familiar with how it is run prior to entry into the setting. Establishing oneself in a setting and familiarizing oneself thoroughly with the equipment will save many headaches once the data collection begins.

REFERENCES

Bowen, E.S. (1964) *Return to Laughter*, Doubleday Inc., New York.

Conners, R.D. (1978) *Using Stimulated Recall in Naturalistic Settings: Some Technical Procedures*, Centre for Research in Teaching, Faculty of Education, The University of Alberta.

Douglas, J.D. (1976) *Investigative Social Research: Individual and Team Research*, Sage Publications, London.

Field, P.A. (1980) 'An Ethnography: Four Nurses' Perspectives of Nursing in A Community Setting', unpublished PhD thesis, University of Alberta, Edmonton.

Germain, C. (1979) *The Cancer Unit: An Ethnography*, Nursing Resources Inc., Wakefield, Massachusetts.

Golde, P. (ed.) (1970) *Women in the Field: Anthropological Experiences*, Aldine Publishing Company, Chicago.

Gregory, J.R. (1984) 'The Myth of the Male Ethnographer and the Woman's World', *Journal of the American Anthropological Association*, 86(2): 316-27.

Kratz, C. (1975) 'Participant Observation in Dyadic and Triadic Situations', *International Journal of Nursing Studies*, 12(3), 169-74.

Morse, J.M. (1984) *Methodology and the Minor Matter of Sampling*, unpublished manuscript, University of Alberta, Edmonton.

Pearsall, M. (1965) 'Participant Observation as a Role and a Method in Behavioral Research', *Nursing Research*, 14(1), 37-42.

Toohey, S. (1984) *Patient-Nurse Interactions in the Emergency Department: An Exploratory Study*, unpublished M.N. thesis, University of Alberta, Edmonton.

Wax, R.H. (1971) *Doing Fieldwork: Warnings and Advice*, University of Chicago Press, Chicago.

Whyte, W. (1955) *Street Corner Society* (2nd edn.), University of Chicago Press, Chicago.

Chapter Five

METHODS OF DATA COLLECTION

Qualitative research encompasses multiple data collection techniques. The major mode of data collection is generally interviewing, often combined with participant observation. Interviewing may be supplemented by open-ended questionnaires, through use of life histories (which may involve oral or written data), diaries, personal collections (letters, photographs), and official documents.

MAJOR METHODS OF DATA COLLECTION

The quality of the research project relies heavily on two skills of the researcher. First is the researcher's ability to obtain information, using both interview and observation methods. To be successful perseverance and sensitivity are critical in order to elicit information from the data during the process of analysis. The techniques of the open-ended interview, the guided interview, the short answer questionnaire and participant observation will be discussed in this section.

INTERVIEW TECHNIQUES

Interviews may be either open-ended or guided. The choice depends upon the amount of knowledge the investigator has relating to the research topic. The major strengths and limitations relating to these types of interviews will be identified.

The Open-Ended Interview

The word 'process' is used deliberately when describing the open-ended interview. It is considered a process because the researcher is exploring new territory with the informant. As this process of exploration develops the interview may be directed by the informant's responses into areas previously unanticipated by the researcher. It is also a process insofar as questions start at a superficial level and increase in depth as relationships within the data are identified. The reader should note that, in qualitative research, the subject is generally referred to as the informant. Alternatively, the terms interviewee or participant may be used.

Gaining Permission. When seeking an interview with an informant the first step is to meet with the prospective participant to discuss the research topic. Discuss the research topic in general terms (e.g., 'breast-feeding', or 'about caring for a diabetic child') rather than 'your attitudes toward breast-feeding', or 'how you manage to control diabetes in a six year old'. The latter examples prematurely delimit the question and bias the information sought from the informant.

Explain that several interviews will be required. Give the informant some idea of how long the interviews will last. As the interview will be tape-recorded the main components of informed consent must be presented (i.e., s/he is free to refuse to answer any questions, may stop the interview and that his/her name will not be associated with the material). As noted in Chapter Three, the informed consent may be obtained at this time or a verbal consent recorded at the beginning of the interview. This preliminary interview is used for the purpose of becoming acquainted and arranging times and places for subsequent interviews.

Minimizing the Dross Rate. During the interview, it is the interviewer's role to guide the interview and to keep the informant on topic. The amount of irrelevant information in an interview is known as the *dross rate*. The dross rate may be high if the informant is an elderly person who is inclined to wander off the topic or if the researcher permits him/herself to be tempted into listening to irrelevant stories or lacks the ability to focus the interview.

The best strategy for minimizing the dross rate is to prepare several open-ended questions before each interview. It is best to begin the first interview with a very broad question, such as 'Tell me about your experiences with juvenile diabetes, when did it begin?' This will enable the researcher to obtain a relatively complete picture of the informant's experiences. The second and subsequent interviews may be more focused on particular methods of coping, or eliciting feelings about the situation.

Establishing Rapport and Developing Trust. The researcher establishes relationships with the informants during the first interview, which will be relatively shallow and polite. The informant will be 'sizing up' the interviewer and making silent decisions about whether or not the interviewer is agreeable and can be trusted. As these barriers are removed the interaction becomes more intimate; the information obtained will then be more valid and more meaningful. The process may be facilitated by the researcher providing a quiet environment, where interruptions will not occur during the interview, by being receptive, and by listening non-judgementally.

Getting Information. It is essential to listen for implicit and explicit meanings in the explanations and descriptions provided by the informant. The interviewer must be able to recognize 'thin' areas and probe for additional information, to remember all that has developed in previous interviews, to make associations and verify assumptions and to 'get inside the informant's skin' so that the topic may be understood from the informant's perspective. This process is exhausting and numbing for both the interviewer and the informant. Therefore, do not continue the interview beyond one hour. Several short interviews are more effective than one long one.

Between interviews the researcher has a lot of work to do. She must listen to the interview, transcribe the interview word for word and plan the direction of the next interview by developing another set of open-ended questions. It is also advisable to examine the transcripts for problem areas in interviewing techniques, for only by careful self-examination can interviewing improve. Seek the assistance of an experienced mentor to assist with evaluation of the quality of the interviews.

The Guided Interview
A guided interview is used when information is required about a topic, when the structure of the topic is known but the answers cannot be anticipated. It is useful because this technique ensures that the researcher will obtain all information required (without forgetting a question), while at the same time permitting the informant freedom of responses and description to illustrate concepts.

Kay (1982) provides an outline for obtaining information cross-culturally on childbirth practices in her book *The Anthropology of Human Birth*. Childbirth is an event in which similar physiological processes occur in a certain order, but the ways in which different cultures respond or manage each of these stages cannot be predicted. Therefore, a guided interview is ideal for obtaining comprehensive and comparable data on birthing practices. As with open-ended interviews, the guided interview is tape-recorded and the responses are transcribed and content analyzed at the end of the interview. Because all respondents have been asked the same questions, responses may be coded, tabulated and descriptive statistics used to examine these data for relationships.

Common Pitfalls in Interviewing
Interruptions. Interruptions by others distract the informant so that thoughts are lost and time must be spent regaining the level of intimacy established prior to the interruption. The most common interruptor is the telephone. If the interview is being conducted in the informant's home, ask if you may unplug the phone, or take the receiver off the hook, so the interview

will not be disturbed.

Select a quiet place where the chance of being overheard is reduced to a minimum. This will assist in the development of rapport and the development of trust with the informant. Often nurse-researchers do not have any choice regarding the place of the interview: the patient is bedfast. If this is the case, inform the staff that, for the next 45 minutes, you wish to interview the patient and place a 'do not disturb' sign on the door. Enquire when medications, treatments or visitors are due so that these times may be avoided. If the patient is in a shared room a separate private place to conduct the interview must be found.

Competing Distractions. A high quality interview will require concentrated energy on the part of both the interviewer and the informant. If while interviewing the interviewer is concerned about making the next appointment, or if the informant is trying to supervise her children, or keep up with a television program, it is not possible to obtain a meaningful interview.

Stage Fright. Stage fright is common to all research where interviews are used to obtain data, but within the qualitative framework it may be increased, not least because of the use of the tape-recorder. An open-ended interview also tends to make the interviewer feel more vulnerable; the tightly structured interview schedule used in quantitative research seems to provide a greater sense of security for the interviewer.

Stage fright may be a problem for the interviewer and/or the informant. The interviewer may have difficulty, especially at first, in 'settling' into the interview. It may be difficult to ask certain questions even though these questions are on the topic that has been preselected for the interview. For example, if the researcher is studying the menopause, cues of discomfort or embarrassment received from the person being interviewed may make the interviewer reluctant to ask questions on such intimate matters. On other occasions, when both the interviewer and the informant are more comfortable, the interview will proceed smoothly.

The second type of 'stage fright' relates to the informant's concern about the use of a tape recorder. As soon as the tape recorder is placed on the table the tone of the informant's voice may change and become artificial. Free exchange stops and the informant suddenly 'doesn't know' or does not have anything to say. The informant may protest that 'her voice sounds awful on tape' or that 'she doesn't have anything to say worth recording'.

There are several strategies to overcome these barriers. The first is to place the tape recorder on the floor, out of sight and use a small pencil, clip-board or lapel microphone to pick up the conversation. Then, as the interview proceeds, the informant 'forgets' about the tape recorder and the interaction quickly becomes normal.

A second strategy is to use telephone inter-views. Ask the informants if they would prefer to be interviewed by telephone, making it clear that the conversation will be recorded. As people are used to speaking on the phone, it is easier for them to speak freely (see Chapter Four).

Occasionally the informant will sense a social distance between him/herself and the researcher. For some, participating in research is a prestigious activity, yet, the notion that a *scientist* is seeking information, asking and listening to what *they* have to say, may be intimidating. In these situations the interview moves slowly and the informant's answers are short and given reluctantly.

When the researcher senses this problem, the best strategy is to 'play dumb'. Ask more probing questions, and respond with surprise or 'you're kidding!' Wax (1971, p. 370) notes that the researcher must 'see himself as an educated and highly intelligent adult, and, simultaneously, as a ludicrous tenderfoot or *schlemiel* who knows less about what he is doing than a native child'. Therefore it is best to accept corrections from the informant as instructive, remembering that learning through laughter and ridicule is an 'ancient if painful method of pedagogy'.

Avoiding Awkward Questions. It is expected that, in the course of an interview, many questions will be asked that are not normally a part of polite conversation. For instance, when studying childbirth or infant feeding it may be necessary to ask about marital status or income level. The informant may feel caught in a bind, not wanting to respond, yet feeling impolite and unhelpful by refusing to answer.

Initially the interviewer should decide if the question is absolutely necessary, given the risks of asking. For example, the informant may be offended by the question and refuse to continue with the interview. As many studies have examined the importance of a support system and the dearth of breast feeding in lower socio-economic classes, a question may be theoretically justified in this breastfeeding example. Risks may be minimized by placing this question last.

Another strategy may be to ask the question in a way which will remove some of the potential embarrassment. Therefore, rather than asking: 'What is your marital status?', the interviewer could ask, 'How many people are living in your household?' The response will provide necessary information regarding the presence or absence of a partner, as well as other people who may provide assistance. Does it matter to the researcher whether or not a couple are married? Remember, the researcher is likely to be interested in *support*, rather than in legal status.

Obtaining information on level of income is trickier. One method would be to write *ranges* of income on a card and ask the informant to identify the range into which the family income falls. As these questions may interfere with the interaction of the interview, if they can be left until last, this should be done.

Jumping. Frequently, interviewers ask questions in an apparently illogical order. For example, when interviewing a mother on her breast-feeding experiences the interviewer may ask about the baby's health at birth, then about the baby's present health. The interview may continue with the initial breast-feeding experiences, then the present breast-feeding experiences; the initial support systems and then the present support systems. While this order makes perfect sense to the interviewer (who has organized the questionnaire for ease of data analysis) this order will not necessarily make sense to the informant. If the mother is trying to explain to the interviewer that her breast-feeding experiences at birth, her present experiences, her initial experiences and her support systems are all interrelated, it may be very difficult for the mother to explain one aspect of the situation at a time. Therefore, the interviewer must elicit the information from the informant's perspective at her own pace.

Usually explaining the experience in chronological order makes most sense in the first interview. Ask the mother to describe breast-feeding experiences from the first time she nursed. In subsequent interviews, when the informant realizes that the interviewer understands the complete picture, comparative questions may be asked.

Frequently the informant is nervous and tries to give the interviewer too much information at once. This is evidenced by rapid speech and disjointed thought processes. Statements such as: 'And before that...' and 'Oh, that was when...' will be indicative of this problem. Stop the interview and ask the informant to tell the story from the beginning. Assure the informant that she has plenty of time and that you will come back for another interview if the story is not finished.

Teaching and Preaching. There is a particular trap for nurses conducting interviews. Quite frequently, about five minutes into the interview, the informant will ask the nurse a question, seeking health information. Immediately the nurse is 'trapped', cannot resist answering and begins doing what we are all trained to do: provide health information! The informant and the interviewer have now switched roles, with the informant now asking the questions and the interviewer responding.

This results in two problems: the first is that the interview is no longer an interview *per se* but a health teaching session. The second is that the interview is changing the informant's knowledge base. For instance, if the researcher is examining lay perceptions of health and giving his/her own opinion on what health is, the lay informant is learning how the interviewer thinks and therefore how subsequent questions should be answered.

When informants are misinformed, or are earnestly seeking health information, this is a slightly different matter. Correct misinformation or answer the questions at the end of the interviewing session, after the information needed for the study has been obtained. Correcting misinformation during the interview not only changes the informant's knowledge, but may inhibit the interaction. Nobody likes to be wrong!

Frequently the informant may ask the researcher a question, not to obtain information, but rather to tell the interviewer something important, which is usually an opinion rather than a fact. This is a strategy used by informants to redirect the interview. Therefore, when a question is asked during an interview, reflect the question back to the informant. Ask, 'Why do you ask?' or 'What is on your mind?' or 'What do you think?' and get at the issues underlying the question.

Counselling. Nurses, in the course of their education, have a great deal of instruction in counselling techniques. They become expert at reflecting and summarizing during an interaction. They frequently use phrases such as, 'Are you saying that...' or 'It seems to me that...'

The use of these techniques too early in the interview or the overuse of these techniques will inhibit the interview, especially if it is on a personal topic. It is easier for the informant to agree with the interviewer than to explain how it *really* is. Preliminary analysis invites premature closure of the topic and precludes in-depth enquiry.

These problems are easy to spot in the typed transcript. There is imbalance in the amount said by the interviewer and the informant. In a good interview the interviewer's responses comprise a much smaller amount of text than the informant's, that is, the bulk of the transcript is description, explanations and clarifications provided by the informant. The interviewer's role is in guiding the direction of the interview, probing, understanding and encouragement. Comfirmation and summarization of information should be left until the end of the interview.

Presenting One's Own Perspective. This is also similar to counselling, teaching and correcting misinformation. When explaining a particular process or event, the informant will look for signs of acceptance or rejection by the interviewer, and use these cues to judge whether s/he should continue. For example, many mothers reject breast-feeding because they feel that it 'really belongs in the barnyard' or is 'animal-like'. Yet these same mothers know that this perspective is not shared by health professionals. Therefore, they may hint at this belief to 'sound out' the interviewer. Frequently these feelers are presented in the third person ('I know that some people think..') or as a friend's belief. If the interviewer takes a position on this belief, for example, by expressing ridicule or disagreement, then the mother will not disclose her true feelings to the interviewer. As the interviewer does not know what the informant really thinks about breast-feeding, the feelings of the interviewer should not be revealed. Rather, s/he should provide an accepting sounding-board for the informant. Do not be trapped by the informant's 'What do you think..?'

Superficial Interviews. We are the best evaluator of the quality of our own interviews. In an interview situation the researcher has the opportunity to assess the non-verbal cues, such as eye contact, facial expression and body posture. As the interview progresses, the interviewer also gets to 'know' the informant, to learn when the informant is uncomfortable answering a question and does not wish to pursue a certain topic, or when s/he is speaking freely.

Frequently interviews are 'shallow' because the interviewer moves the informant along too quickly. The informant does not get time to reflect and explain all aspects of a problem before the interviewer has asked the next question. Using silence, acknowledging with 'hmmm' and giving permission for the informant to continue, is the best way to increase the richness and depth of the data.

Rarely can 'rich' data be obtained from the first interview. Therefore, do not close the relationship with the informant at this time. Rather, ask if it is possible to return if any additional information is needed after the transcript has been reviewed. Interviewing is an exhausting procedure and the interviewer frequently feels drained at the end of an interview. However, after analyzing the tape, many questions and areas that need exploring become obvious and the researcher may need to continue with the interview.

Secret Information. When interviewing, the level of trust may develop between the researcher and the informant to the extent that the informant passes on information labelled as 'secret'. For example, they may state that this is 'Just between you and me..' or 'Don't put this in your report, but...' Alternatively, the informant may provide information that is later regretted. They will state, 'I shouldn't have told you that yesterday..' As the researcher's *first* responsibility is to the informant, the informant has the right to retract information or to request that the information not be used in the report, and the researcher must respect the informant's wishes. Violation of this code will result in loss of trust and may have extensive ramifications for the informant.

However, occasionally information is passed on to the researcher which the researcher feels is the key and is essential for understanding the other pieces in the puzzle. In this case, it is appropriate to recheck to see if the informant will reconsider his/her decision so that the information may be included. Occasionally, a method may be worked out so that the information can be included: if not, forget the information.

Sometimes during the course of an interview the informant will give information to the researcher, which ethically the researcher should 'act on.' Such things as suicide threats are good examples of dilemmas facing a researcher. Our advice is to share with the informant that such matters cannot be kept confidential as life is at risk. Try to persuade the informant to accompany you to seek help. In this way the issue of violation of confidence is faced openly, and hopefully, therapeutically.

The Use of Translators. The use of a translator 'slows' the interview as each statement must be repeated in the alternate language. This is frequently an advantage as it gives the researcher more time to reflect on the previous responses and carefully prepare the next question. It also allows the researcher more time to observe the non-verbal cues of the informant, such as facial expression.

However, there are disadvantages. Firstly, the translator may not accurately translate the affective meaning and expression of the respondent. The translator, rather than providing verbatim responses, may summarize the content of the informant's statements. Secondly, if a semi-structured interview is being conducted, and many people are being interviewed, the translator may become bored with hearing the same answers. Rather than translating the answers, the translator may turn to the researcher and say, 'same as the others' instead of reporting the informant's response.

These problems may be overcome by carefully instructing the translators in the importance of giving complete answers and the correct intonation, and by using more than one translator to prevent boredom.

THE SHORT-ANSWER QUESTIONNAIRE

The short answer, open-ended questionnaire is an appropriate form of data collection to use when some of the dimensions of the construct are known, but all possible responses can not be anticipated. For example, a great deal of research has been conducted on the meaning of health, so that we have some idea about the components of health. But we do not know if lay people view health the same way as professionals and, in order not to 'force' lay definitions into a professional model an open-ended questionnaire could be suitable for this topic.

A second situation in which an open-ended questionnaire would be appropriate is in a situation where interviews may cause embarrassment. For example, this was the ideal method of collecting data on the adolescent's response to menarche (Doan and Morse, In Press). Previous researchers had reported that little information could be obtained using interview methods as the girls were reluctant to express their feelings openly and responded with embarrassed giggles.

The short-answer, open-ended questionnaire takes the form of a short question stem and space, usually one or more blank lines for the respondent to answer the question. As this method of data collection provides some freedom for the responses to the question, these data are more likely to be meaningful and valid. However, the emic or the etic perspective may be obtained depending on the wording of the questions. Consider two similar examples:

(a) Health is: _____

_____

(b) Health, to me, is: _____

_____

Answers to the first question, (a), are likely to resemble known definitions of health, such as the early World Health Organization definition, 'Health is the absence of disease and infirmity', whereas the second question, (b), will elicit an emic definition, such as: 'Health is when you feel good and somebody loves you.'

When constructing an open-ended short-answer questionnaire, it is also important to consider the expected length of the answers and whether a question will require, for example, two lines or six. Respondents tend to write in two-thirds of the required space, whether there are two lines or six lines, and the more they write the more information the researcher obtains. However, there is an upper limit. Too many lines are intimidating and make the questionnaire appear as if it will be too much work and take too much time to complete. The best solution is to pretest the questionnaire. Ask a number of people to complete the questionnaire and examine their answers very carefully to ensure that the type of information required to answer the study question is being obtained. Then ask the respondents to 'critique' the format of the questionnaire for friendliness and effectiveness. While questionnaires of this type are more difficult and time consuming to code than forced-choice questionnaires, they are easier to analyze than an unstructured interview. They have the advantage that the researcher can compare answers to the same questions, and can content analyze and quantify the number of responses in each category for each item.

The major disadvantage of this method is that the respondents must be literate and comfortable expressing their views in writing. The technique would be suitable for use with university students but less suitable for use with blue collar workers. People who hesitate to write because they feel that they cannot spell or people who are unaccustomed to writing will be more likely to refuse to participate in the study; this biases the sample. When English is the informant's second language, although it may be spoken with relative ease, reading comprehension and writing ability in English may be more restricted.

OBSERVATIONAL TECHNIQUES

Information required to answer certain research questions may not be obtained by interviews alone. Data may be obtained solely by observations of the research setting or through a combination of observational and interview methods, known as participant observation. Participant observation is particularly useful in situations in which the researcher needs to verify the information between the informant's reports of behaviour during an actual interview, with the *actual* behaviour that occurs in the setting. Studies on infant feeding practices provide examples to illustrate these discrepancies. Morse (1984) observed that Fijian mothers reported to clinic nurses that they fed their babies every four hours, yet in the village one mother was observed breast-feeding her baby 13 times in three hours. When questioned about this, the mother responded:

> So when I go to see the nurse, they [sic] say, "Do you time your feeds?" and I say, "Yes" and they say, "How often?" and I say, "Every four hours." Then I do whatever I please.

A second type of question that may be answered by participant observational methods is the examination of implicit or unconscious behaviours. For example, Pyles and Stern (1983) examined the ways in which new ICU nurses learned the early detection of cardiogenic shock from a more experienced nurse mentor. The interaction between individuals in the setting may become obvious with observation, whereas informants may not be able to describe such behaviours.

Participant observation also permits the examination of behaviours that may not be included in informants' verbal descriptions of a situation. Observation of patients' gaits, methods of climbing in and out of bed and responses to restraints and side rails provided essential information for a larger study on patient falls (Morse, Tylko and Dixon, in press).

Types of Participant Observation

There are four types of participant observation, classified according to the amount of involvement that the observer has in the research setting (Gold, 1958; Pearsall, 1965).

The types vary according to the amount of participation that the researcher engages in in the setting, from complete participation to complete observer. The primary purposes of participant observation are to observe a *typical* situation, one that is minimally disrupted or altered by the presence of the observer, and to obtain accurate detailed descriptions of the setting. Each type of participant observation is discussed in relation to the facilitation or impediment of this task.

Complete Participation. When conducting complete participation the observer enters the setting as a member of the group and conceals the research role from the group. A nurse interested in observing behaviours in the emergency room would therefore obtain an assignment to that area and not disclose the intent to observe and conduct research to the rest of the emergency room staff.

This type of observation presents the following problems. Firstly, the degree of concealment of the researcher's purpose is rarely defendable. That is, it is a violation of ethical standards to enter a setting and observe in that setting without the knowledge and consent of the participants. Secondly, it is difficult to be immersed in a work role in a setting and to objectively observe at the same time. As a nurse, one must pay attention to the assigned tasks rather than the setting as a whole. Furthermore, it is difficult to find time to make fieldnotes and to conceal this activity from the others. Gold (1958) also notes that the researcher may become so preoccupied with concealing the researcher role that s/he may not perform convincingly in the work role. In addition, after a length of time in the setting, the researcher may 'go native' and lose objectivity and completely adopt the work role, therefore biasing the results.

Participant-as-Observer. In this method the participants in the setting are aware of the researcher's purpose and dual roles. When entering the setting, the researcher usually negotiates work responsibilities with the staff and delineates a small proportion of time for the purpose of writing fieldnotes, observing or conducting formal interviews. This type of observation is suitable if the type of phenomena under study is not constantly present in the setting. For example, the researcher may be interested in post-operative pain and wish to observe patients recovering from anaesthesia. The nurse may elect to assume a work role at times that patients are not available to be observed.

This type of observation has certain disadvantages. Conflict between the two roles may occur when the nurse tries to 'work two jobs at once.' For instance, if the ward becomes busy, the researcher and the staff may feel that the nurse is obliged to assist with the nursing tasks rather than to continue with the research tasks. This may be frustrating to the researcher, especially if the missed research opportunities are a 'rare' event. Ironically, the source of the ward's business is frequently the phenomena in which the researcher is most interested and the difference in priorities may cause conflict on the ward. It is without question, however, that if there is a life-threatening event on the ward, the researcher's first responsibility is to the patient.

Observer-as-Participant. This level of participant observation, with the majority of the researcher's time spent observing and interviewing and minimal participation in the work role, provides more freedom to do research with less conflict. The main disadvantage is that the researcher may be considered an 'outsider' by the staff and not trusted or given access to the insider's perspective of the phenomena. On the other hand, this level of participation may be needed to establish the researcher's credibility in the setting.

Complete Observer. In this role the researcher is passive, having no direct social interaction in the setting. The observer may use one-way mirrors to separate him/herself from the setting, or sit quietly in the corner observing the setting as a 'fly on the wall'. This method has the disadvantage of not permitting the observer to interview, interject or to clarify issues with the participants in the setting. Again, as with the complete participant, concealment behind one-way mirrors without the knowledge of the participants can rarely be justified.

Selecting a Setting
The most frequent mistake that researchers make when doing participant observation is to select a setting in which they already work, or have previously worked, to conduct observations. This will create several problems which will prevent the collection of valid, reliable and meaningful data. Firstly, if the nurse has already established a role or niche in a unit, the staff have certain expectations of that nurse regarding contributions to work. Even negotiating a new role will not remove these expectations, as the staff consider that nurse to be an ally who will help or 'pitch in' if the need arises. Furthermore, as a 'doer' it is hard for the

researcher to sit 'doing nothing' while the staff cannot keep up with the workload. Secondly, the nurse researcher will already be integrated into the group, that is, s/he will be considered a 'native' by those in the setting and have unconsciously incorporated the values of the group to be studied. In this case, it is not possible to be an objective observer.

If the nurse has not been in the setting for some period of time prior to the research, this can be an advantage or a disadvantage. When the nurse re-enters the setting, the period of strangeness and non-comprehension will be reduced so that the nurse will be able to begin meaningful data collection more quickly. However, the period of objectivity before the researcher 'goes native' and has to withdraw from the setting will be shortened considerably. It is important to select a setting in which the researcher will be considered a stranger. This may mean changing hospitals to conduct the research.

Problems with Participant Observation

The major difficulty interfering with validity in participant observation is the change in behaviour in the setting when the observer is present. This change is reduced over time when the participants become used to the observer, feel less threatened, and trust increases.

The researcher must retain the freedom to enter and leave the setting as desired. Do not agree on an 'appointment' system to conduct observations, for this permits the scene to be 'set' for the arrival of the observer. For example, one researcher was observing in a pediatric ward. She was welcomed to make observations 'anytime but bedtime'. The staff thought that observations at bedtime would be disturbing for the children. In actual fact the children's behaviour at this time provided the richest data on separation anxiety.

One method used to verify observations and to overcome this problem is 'spot observation' techniques, as suggested by Rogoff (1978). With this technique the researcher randomly selects times to make observations, and enters the setting unannounced at those times. Katz (In Press), while studying mother-infant interaction in Fiji, used this method. She was interested in the spatial distance between mothers and their infants and made her observations as she entered the household at each randomly selected time.

The second major problem in participant observation is, as mentioned in Chapter Three, the witnessing of unethical behaviours which interfere with patient care. For example, the researcher may observe the slapping of a child, the refusal to give a patient in pain an analgesic, or a bedpan to a patient 'for the 56th time that day'. If the incident is life-threatening there is no question as to the action required. Patient safety is paramount and the researcher intervenes. However, there is a gray area where the researcher knows that if the incident is reported it will result in a role change and the researcher will become a 'policeman' in the view of the patients. If the researcher interferes by getting the bedpan a role change will also occur that will result in a change in the data. No prescriptive advice can be given, for each case depends on individual circumstances. Perhaps, discussing the situation with colleagues or requesting the counsel of the ethics committee will assist in resolving the dilemma.

UNDERSTANDING THE SETTING

As stated, the purpose of data collection and analysis is to enable the researcher to understand the phenomena under study. The first step in understanding is to make sense of the setting or context in which the phenomena are occurring. The use of fieldnotes provides the researcher with both a data gathering and analytical tool to assist with this task.

FIELDNOTES

As it is difficult to remember many details following an observation, there are some critical points to follow when writing fieldnotes to minimize loss of data. These include: getting right to the task; not talking about the observation before it is recorded; finding a quiet place to write; setting aside adequate time to complete the notes; sequencing events in the order they occurred and letting the events and conversation flow from the mind onto the paper. If something is forgotten it can always be added to the notes later.

One point the researcher must consider is that it takes nearly three times as long to record the observation as it does to do the observation. This is one reason why using a tape recorder is preferred as it is faster for the researcher to talk their observations into the recorder.

The Process of Writing Fieldnotes

Fieldnotes consist of jottings of salient points that are reworked in detail later the same day. They take the form of reconstructions of interactions, short conversational excerpts or descriptions of events. The notes recorded during an interaction are kept brief so that the observer can concentrate on what is happening in order to get the feeling of the situation as well as the actual verbal exchange. Fieldnotes are also used to identify ideas on relationships within the data, which then provide a beginning cross check for later analysis.

Fieldnotes are a written account of the things the researcher hears, sees, experiences and thinks in the course of collecting or reflecting on data in a qualitative study (Bogdan and Biklen, 1982). Detailed, accurate and extensive fieldnotes are necessary for a successful qualitative study. In studies which use participant observation all data are recorded as fieldnotes.

Fieldnotes may also be used to supplement other forms of data gathering. A tape-recorded interview does not portray the physical setting, the impressions the observer picks up or the non-verbal communication in an observed interaction. These observations should be recorded in fieldnotes to supplement the taped interview. During the course of the observations the researcher may become aware of subjective biases and unsubstantiated hunches relating to the setting or the phenomena. While some researchers advocate using fieldnotes to record these impressions it may be preferable to record them in a separate diary. In this way objective and subjective records are maintained separately. Furthermore, fieldnotes may become public property and used by future researchers. It is important to keep track of early hunches as they may later prove to be erroneous. Therefore, it is less inhibiting if it is known that these early impressions will remain within the researcher's own files.

The Content of Fieldnotes

As mentioned, fieldnotes are descriptive accounts in which the researcher objectively records what is happening in the setting. The researcher's goal is to capture the lived experience of the participants and to describe the community of which they are a part. It is unrealistic to expect that all aspects of a setting can be described but it is important to record as much as possible in the fieldnotes, guided, in part, by the project's research goals.

In fieldnotes it is necessary to quote what people say rather than to summarize their words. If one is observing a nurse providing care it would be important to describe what that care entailed. For example, an entry may read:

> 'the nurse spoke to the patient, "How are you today, Mrs. B?"', did not wait for a reply, turned back the bedclothes and inspected the dressing'

This provides a more accurate description than saying 'checked the patient'. It is critical not to mix evaluation of actions with a description of care. If the observer stated: 'the nurse made a superficial check', the observer has placed a value on the action by using the word 'superficial'. This leads to the observer glossing over actions rather than dissecting them and searching for the meaning of the action or the reason behind the action.

Fieldnotes will encompass varying areas. The notes may include portraits of subjects, which involve describing physical appearance, dress, mannerisms or style of talking. Any facet of appearance or behaviour which sets an individual apart from the group should be noted.

Another important area to record is reconstruction of dialogue. This resembles nurses' process recordings and may be between participants or may be conversations between participants and the researcher. Both public conversations and private dialogue may be recorded. Non-verbal communication, such as gestures and facial expression should also be noted. When the reconstructed dialogue is only a close approximation of what was said, square brackets, or other selected identifiers, should be used to indicate this in the notes. If it is questionable as to whether or not a passage is accurately recorded this should also be indicated in the notes.

In describing a transcultural situation the researcher may want to make detailed notes of subtle differences in behaviour. For example, the mother may approach bathing a newborn in a way unfamiliar to the observer. A note of the behaviours involved may be needed to recall the details of the activity as once the researcher becomes familiar with the setting such differences may no longer be apparent.

In a hospital setting the relationships among the family may require an account of a particular event. If food is brought by the family, who brings it? Of what does the food consist? Are there rituals to be observed prior to eating? The event, the manner in which the event occurred as well as behaviours specific to the act, should all be recorded.

In another example, Soares (1978), in recording the communication patterns in an intensive care unit, provided details of a communication event. She described the stimulus for the communication, the persons engaged in the communication, the level and tone of voice and the behaviour of the participants. Rich data recorded in the fieldnotes is filled with pieces of evidence that enable the researcher to identify clues that begin to make analytical sense of the data that is studied.

The observer also needs to note any behaviours that may have affected the observation. Actions and conversations, which may have changed the interaction, must be recorded. The influence of the researcher on the setting should be minimized but as there will always be some impact keeping a careful record can help in the assessment of untoward influences.

In addition to descriptive material, the observer may record sentences and paragraphs that reflect a less objective account of the incident and serve as memos. A notation, such as O.C. (Observer's Comment), may be used to identify the observer's feelings, problems, hunches, impressions or prejudices, and any ethical dilemmas or conflicts (Bogdan and Taylor, 1975). The researcher may also indicate areas that need clarification, or potential misunderstandings between the observer and informant.

The Form of Fieldnotes

Fieldnotes may either be talked into a tape recorder for later transcription or recorded in written form. For the latter method a small, neutral-coloured loose-leaf notebook is one of the easiest ways of recording fieldnotes. It is easily portable, and is relatively unobtrusive in use. The notes for each subject can be filed directly into a master file. Dating pages is often of more value than numbering them in keeping track of observations. A second notebook, with pockets, can be used to store consent forms, information sheets, activity sheets and observation and interview schedules, if appropriate. It can also be used to keep track of the progress of the research.

For each separate observation session recorded in the fieldnotes it is wise to record the place the observation took place, the date and time of the observation, who made the observation and the number of this set of notes in the total study (Figure 5.1). This information should be cross-referenced to the researcher's observation and/or interview schedule as this acts as an aid in keeping track of the data and locating related observations or interviews (Figure 5.2).

MAPS

Drawings to show placement of furniture or people during a particular event may also be included in fieldnotes. Physical maps describe arrangements and layouts, physical patterns in the environment and listing of significant objects in a setting. This information may be obtained through observation and through questioning the informants about the significance of observed objects in the setting.

The use of maps in research is particularly appropriate when the movements of persons in social space are relevant to the location and movement of the same persons in physical space (Melbin, 1960). Diagrams (such as socio-grams), floor plans, flow charts and aerial photographs may all be considered maps for research purposes.

For example, in Toohey's (1984) study of an emergency department she demonstrated that the physical structure of the setting allowed the nurses to set the stage in such a way that they appeared to be busy to the patients at times when activity in the emergency department was actually low. The structure also allowed the nurses to avoid sustained contact with patients who were not seen as true emergencies. It was critical to develop maps of the department early in the study in order to identify the relationship between physical and social space.

To summarize, the most general methods of data collection used in

Figure 5.1 Initial Identification on Fieldnotes

Set: 25
P.A. Field

Greenfield Clinic
7 February 1979 2:15 pm
Present: Nurse A.   Mrs. Brown
                                Cindy: 7 months

Date Observation Recorded: 7/2/75

Figure 5.2 Example of Recording of Interview or Observation Schedules

---

Client	Consent	Site	Taped/ Fieldnotes	Date
Corey	P (T)	S	T + F.N. (1)	5 Nov
Corey's Grandma	(W)	H	F.N. (4)	5 Nov
Alfie's Teacher	(T)	S	T (5)	5 Nov
Cindy	P (T)	H	T + F.N.(25)	8 Apr
Charles	(T)	H	T + F.N.(17)	27 Feb
Jeffrey	P (T)	C	T (116)	27 Feb

Observer Shorthand:

P = parents   T = taped   W = written   F.N. = fieldnotes
S = school   H = home   C = clinic

( ) Figures in parentheses indicate the cross reference
to the specific fieldnote

---

qualitative research are interviews, which may be open or semi-structured, coupled with participant observation. When working with very personal topics or with material which may be embarrassing for the subject to talk about to the researcher, open-ended written questionnaires may be used in place of an interview. Telephone interviews may also be employed to decrease the risk entailed when the observer speaks with the researcher in a face to face situation when embarrassing topics are being discussed. Fieldnotes are used to record events and interview data for later analysis.

ADDITIONAL METHODS OF DATA COLLECTION

Life histories, diaries, analysis of personal collections and study of official documents may be used alone or in conjunction with participant observation. Life histories use interviewing techniques and can be considered as a specialized form of interview. Official documents, or hard data such as census information, are used on occasion to verify data provided by informants and may be employed as one method of triangulation.

Life History

A life history is a detailed account of the development of an individual's life over time that enables the researcher to understand the present society in which the individual lives. It can be used to analyze past societies, conditions and circumstances which have contributed to current events. Less comprehensive histories are also of value, if well designed. One form of a life history is the career history of an individual, or in nursing, the health history of an individual may be the focus of interest.

Life histories differ from biographies in that the purpose of a biography is to learn about the details of the life of an individual, usually someone who is well-known in a particular culture or society. The purpose of a life history is to identify a set of common patterns which both the informant and his peers have experienced (Dobbert, 1982). Data obtained for a life history may be gathered in either oral or written form. Life histories may add depth to research in that they add a dimension to understanding that can not be obtained by participant observation alone.

A life history may chronicle an individual's birth, family of orientation, schooling, adolescence, adulthood and the activities of the individual at each stage of development. A life history requires considerable depth and may require a prolonged commitment from the informant if the interviewer is to obtain adequate information. It may be necessary for the researcher to gain access to supporting documents, such as a birth record, school records or marriage certificate if the informant is unsure of dates or facts. Access to documents will depend on the willingness of the informant to provide them or to give consent for the researcher to access them.

Reconstituting one's early years may be difficult. Photographs and other family documents can be used to jar the informant's memory. This type of research requires considerable time commitment and co-operation from the informants.

When obtaining a life history it is critical that the informant's own words be used. Tape recording is normally essential for data collection. However, if tape-recording is not possible nurses have usually had extensive experience process recording interactions and it is appropriate to utilize these skills at this time. One instance where process recording can be used is in the case of an individual whose testimony may put him/her at risk. This would particularly apply if the individual could be recognized from the recorded voice. Languess (1965) elaborates on the ethics of writing a life-history and identifies safeguards for researcher and informant and is a useful reference source for those seeking more detailed information.

An example of the use of life histories in nursing was provided by Larsen (1983) who studied the career histories of ten nurses with Ph.D.s. The major emphasis in this study was on the career patterns of the subjects, but the life histories included information on birth, family orientation, family life, education and the nursing career. Multiple life histories were used to develop a theory of women's career patterns that could be compared to previous theoretical models of men's careers.

Life histories of new immigrants would enable the helping professions to better understand the problems of migration and culture shock. Life histories of some of the early pioneer nurses would add another dimension to the understanding of the evolution of nursing over the last century. The impact of severe or disabling illness on a person's life could be examined through life history techniques.

Diaries

Diaries may be a useful source of data and can provide an intimate descriptive comment on everyday life for an individual. A researcher may use personal diaries that have been kept by an individual on a daily basis. This is a resource that has been used by both historians and biographers to recapitulate and provide insight into an individual's life.

In medical and nursing research, diaries have been used as a means of data collection. The scope of the diaries is generally restricted and the participants are asked to record those things that are of interest to the researcher. Recently, Toumishey (Note 1) asked pregnant women to keep diaries to record the 'minor discomforts' they experienced and their feelings about the pregnancy. Forty women completed diaries, maintaining them over a three month period. This study has not yet been published, but Toumishey reports that through the diaries the subjects have provided many insights into the problems they encountered in pregnancy and their rationale for not seeking medical attention even when the problem seemed to warrant it.

Personal Collections
Personal letters provide rich data that are helpful in revealing relationships between people who correspond. Letters from patients to their families could also provide insights into the hospital experience. Historically many of the published biographies of Florence Nightingale have relied heavily on both her personal and private letters as one source of data for describing her life and career (for example, see Woodham-Smith, 1983).

Personal letters from many individuals may be combined and analyzed to understand an event or phenomenon. The analysis of suicide notes (Lester and Reeve, 1982) is an example of this type of research.

Official Documents
In health care research the most commonly used type of official documents are vital statistics, health care statistics, hospital statistics and patient/client records. Hospitals and health care agencies keep and generate tremendous amounts of qualitative and quantitative data. Quantitative data, such as patient statistics, can be useful in showing trends in care. Statistics may also be used to support the representativeness of the informants in a qualitative study in relation to the social group being studied when this information is of use. Statistical data may also be used to check impressions. For example, if the observer in an outpatient setting sees very few children, this observation can be checked against attendance statistics, thus validating the observation. The researcher might then seek for an explanation of this finding: 'Why do few children attend outpatients for care?'

In qualitative research patient records can also be used to validate information provided by patients and nurses about treatment or medical intervention on a given unit. Charts may also be the primary unit of analysis for qualitative researchers interested in examining certain trends. One example would be an analysis of Kardex to explore the 'labels' nurses give to patients.

Other official documents may be formal admission or discharge interviews. Cohen (1981) studied students who left nursing without completing an educational program. She compared entry grades and school marks with five years of exit interviews and found underachievement was related to emotional problems and an inability to accept the nurse's role and not to a lack of intellectual potential.

OTHER APPROACHES

Case Studies

A case study may be a detailed examination of a single subject, a single setting, a single set of documents or one particular event. Thus, an ethnographic study of a community, a hospital unit, a family, or a patient may be considered a case study.

A case study generally starts with broad objectives and moves to a narrower focus as the study progresses (Bogdan and Biklen, 1982). According to Deising (1971, pp. 227-88) a problem in the research design of a case study is delineating the boundaries of the research entity. Traditionally, researchers selected the natural boundaries of the system. For example, early anthropologists would select a village or a small tribe, which was geographically or linguistically distinct, and studied the entire unit. As knowledge increased, research techniques developed, and research questions changed, the required work to complete this task became impossible and the ideal holistic analysis of a setting became increasingly unrealistic.

As research was carried out in increasingly complex societies and situations it became necessary for the unit of analysis for the case study to be more focused. Traditional boundaries changed and it became evident that the delineation of the research topic had to be artificial, both laterally in space and linearly in time. The costs of ignoring the lateral contexts is illustrated by the researcher focussing on a hospitalized patient and ignoring the patient's family and home environment, colleagues and work environment, friends and recreational activities — in short, his/her life outside the patient role. The costs of ignoring the lineal-temporal context is to ignore both past events leading to the patient's present situation and the patient's future plans and aspirations.

Such a narrow approach is unacceptable. It is up to the researcher to decide on the extent of the compromise needed in relation to the depth of study and to consider the lateral and lineal contexts needed for the study.

Koos (1954) used a case study approach to find out what people thought and did about their health. The study covered a five year period and involved family interviews with families throughout a community which he called 'Regionville'. The unit of the township made it geographically distinct while the focus of the study was limited to the health of the population. The time frame and the questions asked of the families both considered the lineal-temporal context of health. This is regarded as a classic case study in field research.

Historical Organizations. A case study of an organization examines a particular organization over time. It traces the organization's development, examining changes. In a study of a culture, the elders' perspective of life when they were a child compared with current values and structure of society would enable the researcher to understand cultural change. This can be a useful form of gathering data in studying, for example, problems of acculturation.

Sociologists may use the historical organization approach in examining the introduction of new technology and the changes this creates in the work situation. If such a study is to be done retrospectively it would be critical to determine what documents have been preserved and who was available to interview to provide the long-term perspective needed for this type of research.

Multiple Site Research

By using the case study method simultaneously in two or more settings, it is possible to compare and contrast the settings. This method doubles the researcher's work, but the constant comparison of the two settings provides richness of data and important insights for theory development.

Team Research

The problem of increased workload may be partially overcome through the use of several researchers. The members of the team are all involved with the planning of the research, and the collection and the analysis of data. Therefore, excellent and frequent communications between team members regarding the focus of the study, the content of interviews and emerging categories is essential. If an attitude of free exchange is not present, then the quality and the quantity of the research is impaired.

Douglas (1976) writes of several advantages of the team approach. Most importantly, many of the barriers to interviewing may be removed. For example, both sides of a conflict situation may be obtained or the sex bias of interviews can be removed by male interviewers interviewing male informants. The consideration of 'working up' through a social organization is partly removed by instructing one team member to interview 'the bosses' and one team member to interview 'the workers', also by using this approach the length of time for data collection may be reduced. Nevertheless, this does not reduce the cost of the total project as more interviewers must be used.

Finally, as mentioned in Chapter Two, the method of research chosen depends on the maturity of the concept and the type of research questions being asked. In selecting the approach to be used in collecting data the researcher must consider what is feasible, how the question may best be answered and the goals of the research.

The discussion of the modes of data collection is not exhausted in this chapter. Researchers may be able to develop unique observational situations and find untapped sources of data for their own studies. It is always essential for researchers to think through the sources of error and threats to validity and reliability when a unique or untried approach is used.

REFERENCES

Bogdan, R.C. and Biklen, S.K. (1982) *Qualitative Research for Education: An Introduction to Theory and Methods*, Allyn and Bacon, Boston.

Bogdan, R.C. and Taylor, S.J. (1975) *Introduction to Qualitative Research Methods: A Phenomenological Approach to the Social Sciences*, John Wiley & Sons, New York.

Cohen, H.A. (1981) *The Nurse's Quest for a Professional Identity*, Addison-Wesley Publications, Menlo Park, California.

Deising, P. (1971) *Patterns of Discovery in the Social Sciences*, Aldine Publishing Co., New York.

Doan, H. and Morse, J. 'Roadblocks for Researching Menstruation', *Health Care for Women International*, in press.

Dobbert, M.C. (1982) *Ethnographic Research*, Praeger Special Studies, Praeger Publishers, New York.

Douglas, J. (1976) *Investigative Social Research: Individual and Team Research*, Sage, California.

Gold, R.L. (1958) 'Roles in Sociological Observation', *Social Forces*, 36, 217-23.

Katz, M. 'The Relation of Mothers' Roles and Resources to Infant Care in the Outer Fiji Islands' in L. Marshall (ed.), *Infant Care and Feeding in Oceania*, Gordon and Breach, New York, in press.

Kay, M. (1982) *The Anthropology of Human Birth*, F.A. Davis, Philadelphia.

Koos, E.L. (1954) *The Health of Regionville: What People Thought and Did About It*, Columbia University Press, New York.

Languess, L.C. (1965) *The Life History in Anthropological Science*, Holt, Rinehart & Winston, New York.

Larsen, J. (1983) *A Psychosocial Study of the Career Development of Selected Nurses with Earned Doctoral Degrees*, unpublished PhD thesis, Faculty of Education, University of Alberta.

Lester, D. and Reeve, C. (1982) 'The Suicide Notes of Young and Old People', *Psychological Reports*, 50, 334.

Melbin, M. (1960) 'Mapping Uses and Methods' in R.N. Adams and J.J. Preiss (eds.), *Human Organization Research: Field Relations and Techniques*, Dorsey Press Inc., Homewood, Illinois, pp. 255-66.

Morse, J.M. (1984) 'Cultural Context of Infant Feeding in Fiji', *Ecology of Food and Nutrition*, *14*, 287-96.

Morse, J.M., Tylko, S. and Dixon, H. 'Identifying the Fall-Prone Patient', Proceedings of the Tenth National Canadian Nurse Researchers Conference, Toronto, Ontario, in press.

Pearsall, M. (1965) 'Participant Observation as a Role and Method in Behavioral Research', *Nursing Research*, *14*(1), 37-42.

Pyles, S.H. and Stern, P.N. (1983) 'Discovery of Nursing Gestalt in Critical Care Nursing: The Importance of the Gray Gorilla Syndrome', *Image: The Journal of Nursing Scholarship*, *15*(2), 51-7.

Rogoff, B. (1978) 'Spot Observation: An Introduction and Examination', *Institute for Comparative Human Development*, *2*(2), 21-6.

Soares, C.A. (1978) 'Low Verbal Usage and Status Maintenance Among Intensive Care Nurses', in N.L. Chaska (ed.), *The Nursing Profession: Views Through the Mist*, McGraw-Hill, New York (pp. 198-204).

Toohey, S. (1984) *Parent-Nurse Interactions in the Emergency Department: An Exploratory Study*, unpublished M.N. thesis, University of Alberta, Edmonton.

Wax, R. (1971) *Doing Fieldwork: Warnings and Advice*, University of Chicago Press, Chicago.

Woodham-Smith, C. (1983) *Florence Nightingale 1820-1910*, Atheneum, New York.

Note 1

Toumishey, H. Personal communication on work in progress. Memorial University, St. Johns, Newfoundland, April 1984.

Chapter Six

THE PROCESS OF ANALYZING DATA

One of the most striking differences in data collection and analysis between qualitative and quantitative approaches is the process-orientation in qualitative research and the 'one-shot' nature of data collection and analysis in quantitative research. In this chapter, the process of data collection and analysis used in qualitative research will be described and issues associated with this process, such as reliability and validity, will be discussed.

THE PROCESS OF DOING FIELDWORK

During the process of data collection the quantity and the quality of the data collected varies according to the relationship of the researcher to the setting. The process of fieldwork (researcher comprehension, observer objectivity, data collection and analysis) will be discussed in relationship to the four stages of data collection (negotiating entry, selecting informants, acceptance and cooperation, and withdrawal from the setting) (see Figure 6.1).

In Phase I, negotiating entry, the collection of data begins although the quality of data obtained is poor. Due to the stress of entry (as described in Chapter Four) the researcher has low comprehension of the setting and the research question may still be unfocussed. In spite of these problems, as data collection is the primary mechanism used for interpreting the setting and developing a focus for study, data analysis begins soon after entry.

During the second phase, acceptance of the researcher is increased and the data collected become more significant until Phase III (acceptance and cooperation) is attained during which time data collection is efficient and focussed. In this phase, researcher comprehension, effectiveness and objectivity is maximal. During this period, the emerging theory hopefully 'falls into place'. Occasionally the researcher may encounter some difficulty making sense of the data. If this occurs the researcher may either take a break to distance him/herself from the data, or discuss the data with a colleague to obtain a fresh perspective. Alternatively, if it is not possible to bounce ones ideas off a colleague, explain the emerging ideas to an interested friend. This process of explanation frequently

Figure 6.1 The Stages of Fieldwork

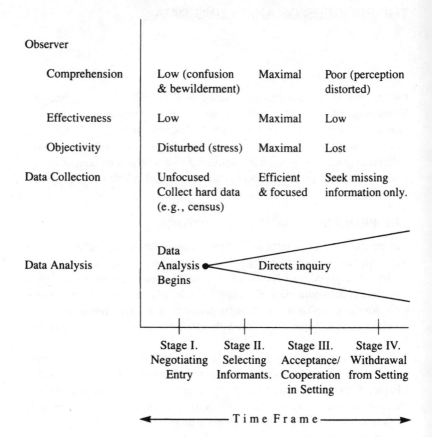

clarifies one's own thinking.

As time progresses the researcher may become too close to the informants and become a part of the group, or 'go native'. When this happens, the researcher becomes an ally of the informants so that perception becomes distorted and effectiveness and objectivity are lost. At this point the theory should be developed sufficiently for the researcher to focus on obtaining missing information to fill in gaps in the developing theory and for confirming the theory. The researcher prepares to leave the setting.

The length of time that the researcher takes to comprehend the setting and the period within which the researcher can work effectively and efficiently depends upon the similarities between the researcher and the participants. For instance, if the researcher is a neonatal ICU specialist and the site of the study is a neonatal ICU, the length of time before comprehension is reached will be relatively short. In addition, the length of time available for data collection before objectivity is lost will be considerably shorter than if a non-nurse, unfamiliar with the setting, was conducting the research. Furthermore, it is the absence of objectivity that prohibits the conduct of research in one's own work environment, with one's own family or any other setting in which the researcher has an established role and identity. The first task in any setting is the selection of informants, a task that is accomplished after entering the setting.

SAMPLING PROCEDURES

While there is an apparent feud between qualitative and quantitative research perspectives, in reality research cannot easily be separated into these two categories. It is better to perceive research methods on a continuum ranging from phenomenology to experimental research in a controlled laboratory setting. Between these two extremes the level of measurement and the purpose of research merge into a grey area in which most of the sampling problems (and research disagreements) occur.

One must remember that the purpose of quantitative research is to examine the distribution of previously known phenomena in a population, testing the relationship between variables. Given the purpose of the study it is appropriate that random sampling techniques be used. On the other hand, the qualitative researcher seeks to understand phenomena. The information about such phenomena may not be evenly distributed in a population (Agar, 1980, pp. 120-1). For example, if one wants to understand the culture of Grade IX girls, as in Davis' study (1972) the population immediately becomes circumscribed and techniques of random sampling become inappropriate. Some informants or interviewees may be gate-keepers to certain aspects or domains of knowledge, while others may know less due to lack of experience, lack of access to specialized knowledge, lack of perceptivity and so forth. One selects the sample because of the purpose of the study rather than because of the relationship of the subjects to the overall structure of the group.

Consider the library as analogous to a population to illustrate this point. If the student wishes to 'know something' then inquiry is directed, using the card catalogue and indexes, to the relatively few books or journals containing the information. However, if something is to be known about the library books, such as the number of female authors, or the average number of pages in books, then selecting a random sample of books is appropriate.

The qualitative researcher must clearly delineate the characteristics of the participants and their place in the social setting. Information may change over time. How adolescents describe their experience of adolescence will be different from the way in which elderly females describe their experience of adolescence. One has only to survey the trends in adolescent clothes and behaviour over the last three decades to recognize the rapid shift in adolescent cultural values that occur over relatively short time spans. Knowing the circumstances and the informants helps to account for disagreements in different accounts of the same culture.

The reluctant informant can be compared to the 'non-response rate' in quantitative research. Such bias must be identified but some lack of response is to be expected and may be acceptable as falling within 'normal' limits. Clear description of those refusing to participate in the study, or the circumstances that created any failure to obtain information, will increase the credibility of the study.

Another problem in qualitative research is predicting the required sample size. Data are collected until no new information is obtained. When writing the report, the researchers should be able to describe or justify the final sample size but may not be able to predict the required sample size beforehand.

Types of Samples
The main types of sampling methods used in qualitative research are described below:

Opportunistic Sample. When using an opportunistic sample, informants are selected according to the quality of their relationship with the researcher and their ability to articulate and to provide explanations for the researcher (Agar, 1980, p. 120). Note that this type of sampling differs from a *convenience sample* (Diers, 1979, p. 86) which may be limited by time constraints or other factors.

Judgmental Sample. This term is used to describe the process of seeking out informants because of their specialized knowledge of some particular topic (Agar, 1980, p. 120).

Purposeful (or Purposive) Sample. In this sampling design informants who will most facilitate the development of the emerging theory are selected (Bogdan and Biklen, 1982, p. 67; Diers, 1979, p. 86). Such informants have specific characteristics or knowledge which will add to, support or refute (i.e., negative cases) the theory, thus enhancing the researcher's understanding of the setting. In grounded theory this type of sampling is known as *theoretical sampling* (Glaser and Strauss, 1967; Glaser, 1979).

Snowball or Nominated Sample. With snowball, or nominated, sampling, the researcher first establishes trust with an informant (Bogdan and Biklen, 1982, p. 66; Diers, 1979, p. 87). When the interviews with that informant are completed, the informant is asked to introduce or refer the researcher to another person to interview. Thus, the sampling frame follows social networks. Although 'biased', this technique is particularly useful when the researcher is regarded with suspicion and distrust in the setting.

Quota Sample. In the case of a quota sample, the sampling design is organized according to ba priorie categorizations set by the researcher (Diers, 1979, p. 87). For example, the researcher may decide that the experience of managing a colostomy is different for people depending on age and sex, and, therefore, decide to justify the sampling frame by interviewing five elderly male, five elderly female, five young female, and five young male new colostomy patients and making comparisons between each of these four categories. However, using this type of sampling frame removes the inductive analytical power of qualitative research and must be used with caution.

Random Sample. This method of sampling ensures that everyone in the population has an equal chance of being included in the study (Agar, 1980, p. 120; Bogdan and Biklen, 1982, p. 66; Diers, 1979, pp. 82-5). Thus, the sample is considered to be 'representative' and the findings unbiased and generalizable. However, as stated, it is not the purpose of qualitative research to comment on the distribution frequency in a population (how many or in what proportion), but rather to ensure that many types are included in the sample for the purposes of developing theory.

Thus random sampling is usually inappropriate (Bogdan and Biklen, 1982, p. 67). Furthermore, Agar (1980, p. 121) notes that blindly sticking to a sampling frame when, for example, one-third of the informants may be giving poor information is a 'pointless ritual adherence to a procedure without concern for the goals [of the research]'.

Sampling Events. In participant observation events may be observed by direct observation, or by using hypothetically created situations (Agar, 1980, p. 126). For example, if the researcher is interested in positions women adopt in labour, this information may be obtained, of course, by observing births. If, however, a birth in the community is not a frequent event, the researcher may also obtain this information by asking women to 'act' or to demonstrate the position that they use to give birth. Observations of several independent and consistently similar positions will indicate that the hypothetically created situations probably represent the actual event.

Spot Observations. The purpose of spot observation techniques is to ensure that reported behaviours are typical behaviours (Rogoff, 1978). Observation times are randomly selected and the researcher makes observations at those selected times (see Chapter Five).

In qualitative research the data are collected and analyzed concurrently. As the researcher gains insight into the research problem the question may refocus and new questions and hypotheses may arise to be tested. These progressions dictate and change sampling procedures. Furthermore, the rephrasing of the question ensures the answers are valid in relation to the changing focus. Careful description of the way in which sampling evolved and questions changed is a critical part of reporting the research.

DATA ANALYSIS

The initial analytic process is imbedded in the process of recording and analyzing fieldnotes and interviews. The analytic task of making sense out of the data in a qualitative research study may seem to be a monumental task for the beginning researcher. There are many different styles of qualitative research and many different approaches to handling the data, but similar processes are involved and analysis takes place in an orderly fashion. Data, in qualitative analysis, are usually in the form of narrative text derived from transcribed interviews, written descriptions of observations in fieldnotes and reflections on the dynamics of the setting in the researcher's diary. These records may be voluminous. A 45-minute interview, for instance, may result in 25 pages of text to be coded, sorted, analyzed and stored in a form that may be easily retrieved.

Managing such a data base is an immense task, which may be fraught with frustration when attempting to 'make sense' of the data while, at the same time, endeavouring to locate a description to illustrate a particular concept or event. The purpose of data analysis is, therefore, twofold. The first purpose is to code the data so that the categories may be recognized, analyzed and behaviours noted. The second is to develop a data filing system that will provide a flexible storage system with procedures for retrieving the data. It is our experience that some new researchers have been dissatisfied with 'set' instructions for analyzing data and have developed their own. General principles will be described, rather than presenting rigid procedures.

Transcribing Fieldnotes
When transcribing fieldnotes the use of spaced paragraphs and wide margins makes data coding simpler. Start a new paragraph each time a topic is changed. Large margins to the left of the page allow room for notation and coding.

In the example shown in Figure 6.2, the initial description of the setting, the observer's comments (O.C.) and the time of onset of the interview are shown. In this case the margin is not marked, but a pencilled in margin is equally acceptable.

As a researcher becomes more experienced at ongoing analysis, notes tend to become shorter and fewer in number. The most extensive notes are usually taken at initial visits, during which time the study will still be relatively open and unfocussed. The focus of the fieldnotes will generally be dictated by the purpose of the study.

Transcribing Interviews
The first major task in analyzing interview data is to become extraordinarily familiar with the data. As soon as possible after the completion of a tape recorded interview, the tape should be replayed with the researcher listening carefully to the questions and to the tone of the responses as well as to the content. As noted previously in Chapter Five, fieldnotes are written at this time to describe the interview context.

It is not possible to analyze a tape without a written transcript. The tape is therefore transcribed word for word either by the investigator or a typist. Pauses are denoted in the transcript with dashes, while series of dots indicate gaps or prolonged pauses. All exclamations, including laughter and expletives, are included. Instruct the typist to type interviews single-spaced with a blank line between speakers. A generous margin on both sides of the page permits the left margin to be used for coding and the researcher's own critique of the interview style, and the

Figure 6.2 Example of Fieldnotes

Margin Left for Coding	I arrived at the home, a well kept stucco, two storey house at 2pm. The house was in an older area and an addition had been made to the house.
	The family, Mrs. A., her sister and two children, were in the garden. The sister said she would watch the children. Mrs. A. invited me into the house. She offered me a cup of tea, which I accepted.
	O.C. Mrs. A. seemed relaxed in contrast to the time I had seen her in the hospital.
	Researcher: Can you describe your child's injury?
	Mrs. A.: Most definitely. He was playing ball in the back yard here and was running to catch the ball and ran into the back gate cutting open his head - we think he hit it on the latch - it was kind of freakish because it must have been the way he fell on his head.

right margin to be used for comments regarding the content. Transcribing is a time consuming task and the researcher needs to invest in a transcriber if time is to be used efficiently.

Following the transcribing of the interview, replay the tape again. After transcribing check to see that the transcription was accurate and insert margin notes. Changes in voice or tone, significant pauses and inflections which may indicate that the topic is highly important, or emotionally charged, become lost in transcribing. Notations need to be made on the transcript by the researcher. Ensure all pages are numbered sequentially and that each page is coded with the interview number and the informant's number, as illustrated in Figure 6.3.

One of the most serious mistakes made by the novice researcher is to skimp on the duplication of the transcripts. At this stage, make at least three copies and separate the original from the working copies. Keep one set of transcripts locked in a different location as insurance against loss or fire damage. If working in the field, mail one copy home separately when travelling; do not place it all together in one suitcase. Lost data at this stage is disastrous!

Methods of Coding

By this time the researcher will be able to recognize the persistent words, phrases, themes or concepts within the data. The task becomes one of identifying these words, passages or paragraphs for later retrieval.

One way to do this is to use a highlighter pen, using a different colour for each of the major categories. A second method, first used by Murdock (1971) is to develop a list of all major categories and assign these major categories a number. This method is also well illustrated by Miles and Huberman (1984, p. 61). The assigned number is then inserted into the text to identify appropriate content. For example, in a study of adolescents' anticipated responses to menstruation (Morse and Doan, 1984), one girl wrote:

> I am going to feel embarrassed (43). If I have it when my mom isn't around, I won't tell my dad (26) (31) (32). I would be embarrassed (43).

In this example, the code 43 indicates a category, 'embarrassment,' code 26 indicates that the girl had made plans for coping in advance of the onset of menstruation, code 31 indicates plans to reveal menstruation to mother, but code 32, to conceal menstruation from her father.

Another method is to write the major categories in the margins and then to sort the data by cutting and pasting or by copying the relevant passage onto cards for manual sorting (see Data Filing Systems).

Figure 6.3 Example of Transcript with Researcher's Notes Added

Interview: 27/10/79
Page #5
Informant #63 #65
Nurse A

Transcript of Observed Interview	Researcher's Notations
#63 C. You've been taking drugs.	Voice sounds accusing
#65 V. Holy Mother of God! — so strike me dead if I am lying! I had whiskey.	V. crosses herself
Nurse A Charles, I can understand you worrying about Vivian and pills but she is only getting angry when you ask.	Nurse (A) sitting between C. & V. Researcher in chair to left; calm voice
#63 C. Damn right she is. She'll deny it and deny it but I know she's had pills. Look at her — she's high. Whiskey — she don't smell of whiskey....	Bangs fist on table. Points to V.
#65 V. I gave up drugs. He can give up whiskey.	Looks straight ahead voice flat, quieter.
#63 C. She was on heroin. You should see her arms — black they are — but she gave that up. It's those prescriptions — librium.	Voice raised on last sentence
#65 V. Give up drinking. I need pills for my nerves. The doctor says so. You're an alcoholic.	Command tone. Emphasis on "you're"
#63 C. Vivian you have been taking pills — I know you have.	
#65 V. I haven't — so help me God. My dad gave up alcohol cold, ten years before he died. What's she doing - She's not talking. Is she a spy?	Points to researcher. Gets up to look.

Categories are initially as broad as possible without overlapping. Therefore, few categories are chosen in the initial stages of the analysis. Then, as more information is compiled on each topic, the major categories may be sorted into smaller categories. This is the 'rule of parsimony' and enables the data to remain manageable, permits sub-categories to be derived from the larger domain and the researcher to remain mentally stable. Experience has shown that it is difficult during the initial data coding stage to work with more than ten major codes.

DATA FILING SYSTEMS

There are two major approaches to setting up data filing systems. The first approach is to use some form of manual method; the second, more recent development, involves the use of the computer to set up a data filing system.

Manual Methods

The simplest method for data analysis is the use of highlighting pens which leaves the typed page intact. This method, however, cannot be used with extensive data sets. It is not possible to adequately code all the pages and to retrieve the required passages which quickly become voluminous when multiple interviews are involved. Analysis of categories within the major constructs is extremely difficult, perhaps even impossible, with this technique. This method, therefore, is not recommended for larger studies and may be problematic even when small amounts of data are involved.

The second method has been used by anthropological field workers for generations. Concepts or quotes are copied onto cards and these are filed under the appropriate category. McBee cards (cards with holes punched in the top) allow easy retrieval and permit the cards to be filed under more than one category if needed. The holes pertaining to the data categories, recorded on the cards, are left intact and those categories that are not used are punched out. Retrieval is made with a metal skewer and all cards containing the selected category may be lifted from the data set.

Goffman was rumoured to use a similar card system. It is said that he transcribed fieldnotes onto cards and sorted these cards by placing them in large brown envelopes. These envelopes were labelled (one per category) and pinned all over his office walls. Apparently, when an envelope became heavy enough to fall off the wall, there was enough data to sort into sub-categories.

A third method and the one most frequently used by the present writers, is to colour code each page of the interview in the left margin. Use one coloured stripe for each participant, and another for the interview

(1st, 2nd or 3rd, etc.). Then, when analyzing the data, cut the significant passages from the interview, tape each piece onto a full size sheet of paper and file it in the appropriate folder for that category. The colour coding is a fast method of identifying all data, allowing pieces coded for analysis to be traced to the original source. Cutting the transcript enables the data to be quickly sorted without the necessity of rewriting the appropriate passage onto another card. However, as one segment may fit into two or more categories, the need for several copies of data is obvious. As the file folders fill, the contents are again sorted into smaller categories.

Computer Analysis

The recent microcomputer revolution may remove many of the disadvantages of manual methods of data analysis (Kirk, 1981; Sproull and Sproull, 1982). Data may be entered directly by transcribing from the audio tape into the file. Later the data can be coded and retrieved without being removed from the total interview. Data are less likely to be 'lost', as is possible with the cutting and pasting procedures or with card sorts. Furthermore, as Podolefsky and McCarty (1983, p. 887) note, data can also be searched for uncoded categories (such as places or events) if a unique identifier can be used.

Data entry techniques may be extraordinarily simple. Interviews or fieldnotes are directly transcribed into the computer, using approximately two-thirds of each computer line. For instance, if the microcomputer is set to 80 columns, use only 60 columns for the text and leave 20 columns for codes, or, if using a mainframe with 120 columns, use 80 columns for the text and add 40 columns for codes. As data are entered, separate 'topics' or paragraphs with a blank line.

After these data are entered, obtain a printout of the text and code and enter these codes into the computer on the appropriate line within each paragraph, including the informant and the interview numbers. Then, using the text editor, it is possible to search for a particular code, or informant, or interview. It is also possible to obtain printouts by informant or to obtain information across interviews or across informants for comparative purposes.

The previous example of data coding is presented again, this time coded as it would be for the computer file:

    76 12 I am going to feel embarrassed 43

    76 12 If I have it when my mom 26 31 32

    76 12 isn't around, I won't tell my 26 31 32

    76 12 dad. I would be embarrassed. 26 31 32 43

In the left hand column the first set of numbers is the informants code; the second set the page of the interview. The numbers on the right hand side of the page are the previously mentioned coding categories.

TYPES OF CONTENT ANALYSIS

In recent years the types of content analyses have proliferated. Phenomenologists write of thematic analysis (analyzing for themes), linguists of semantic analysis (analyzing the language) and others of content analysis (analyzing for categories, constructs, domains and so forth). Lofland (1971) makes a useful distinction between static and phase analysis. A static analysis will depict an event as it occurs. Phase analysis is used to trace the development of a phenomenon over a period of time. It is important for the researcher to use both forms of analysis and to identify the two processes when reporting the research. Furthermore, it is necessary to link static events with one another and to demonstrate relationships between such events if they exist.

Fox (1982, pp. 391-409) and Babbie (1979, p. 279) write of latent and manifest content analysis. Latent content analysis is the type most commonly used in qualitative analysis. Passages or paragraphs are reviewed within the context of the entire interview in order to identify and code the major thrust or intent of the section and the significant meanings within the passage. This permits the overt intent of the informant to be coded, in addition to the analysis of the underlying meanings in the communication. Thus the method has high validity, but may be less reliable due to the possible subjective nature of the coding system.

When using manifest content analysis the researcher surveys the transcripts for words, phrases, descriptors and terms central to the research topic. These are tabulated and may be analyzed using descriptive statistics. The numeric objectivity of the analysis increases the reliability of the procedure, but loses validity as the technique denies the richness of the data and the research context.

Frequently researchers use both methods in a complementary fashion. They may start with thick description and latent content analysis as categories are established and described, then move on to tabulation and descriptive statistics to enumerate the number of times specific concepts were discussed or behaviours observed. Care must be taken when this technique is employed as factors such as time, verbal expressiveness or repetitions may influence the number of instances of a phenomenon being observed and in qualitative research these variables are not constant for all participants.

CLASSIFICATION SYSTEMS

In the initial phase of the analysis the researcher attempts to identify the characteristics of observed phenomena. In making notations, the researcher should note:

>   i) the kind of things that are going on in the context being studied;
>   ii) the forms a phenomenon takes; and
>   iii) any variations within a phenomenon.

The purpose of this analysis is to delineate the form, kinds, and types of social phenomena and to document their existence. This is the naming process that results in the development of classification systems. One example of the use of a taxonomy is the Linnean (taxonomy) used to classify living organisms. Each category of lifeform has a list of characteristics that allows scientists to place all living objects within the classification system. A taxonomy does not, however, account for processes. A taxonomy or classification system, whose function is to name objects, only creates an orderly framework for analyzing the data. Within a given setting acts (one-shot events), activities (ongoing events), verbal productions that direct actions (meanings), participation of the actors, interrelationships among actions and the setting of the study may all be means of setting up a classification system.

In the anthropological tradition, the history, social structure, recurring events, economy, authority, beliefs and values of a community may constitute the initial list of universal categories used to organize data. On the other hand, categories may arise easily from the data. For example, in a study of patient satisfaction with nursing care, when the informant says: 'Oh, the nurses were great but the interns - they were another matter', one already has as categories 'nurses' and 'interns'. The behaviours 'were great' and the alternative 'were another matter' indicate two areas which the researcher needs to explore further in order to understand the meaning of these phrases for the informant. From the start, the researcher will be able to record labels for categories provided by informants. If a category of 'doctors' emerges 'interns' will become a segregate or subset of that category.

Matrix Formation

In examining the universals it may be useful to develop matrices to look at relationships between categories. Development of a matrix may help to uncover the relationships between parents and the sick child, the role the nurse and physician play in this relationship (authority, decision making) and the meanings conveyed by covert rules. It may be noted that the categories developed can be related to established theoretical concepts such as kinship, group ritual and authority, but use labels that match the data as closely as possible. To note such relationships may be valuable in formulating tentative propositions and in interpreting the data. Spradley (1980, p. 82-3) provides an excellent example of questions developed to describe a phenomenon. This example graphs all possible relationships along the dimensions of space, object, act, activity, event, time, actor, goal, and feeling so that a comprehensive picture of all possible relationships is obtained.

Formulating Tentative Propositions
As the fieldworker collects more data, relationships among behaviours, participants, activities and so forth, will begin to emerge. The researcher will develop hunches about relationships within the data and will formulate tentative propositions about these relationships. In some studies one will see the term 'proposition' used, while in others research hypotheses will be generated. A proposition is: a subject to be discussed or a statement to be upheld. It is something to be assumed for the purpose of argument. A hypothesis is defined as: a proposition or principle which is supposed or taken for granted in order to draw a conclusion. It is a theoretical relationship between variables imagined or assumed for the purpose of argument. The choice of term would seem to be more a matter of training than of real difference.

Propositions are stated in such a way that they indicate potential relationships within the data. They may be stated as causal propositions. For example, a study on clients who attended a nurse-run clinic, where the goal was health promotion, yielded the following propositions (Field, 1984):

1. clients who perceive themselves as having inner control over their daily activities will expect guidance and support from the nurse in response to their initiation of an interaction; and

2. clients who lack inner control over their daily activities will expect the nurse to act as an authoritarian figure who exerts control.

These propositions are then used to guide further data gathering. The researcher looks for supporting evidence and for evidence that will disprove the proposition or hypothesis. Tentative propositions may be supported, may have to be amended, or may need to be discarded over the course of a study. Hypotheses are a necessary part of the research process when qualitative data is to be converted to quantifiable data for analysis or if new theoretical ideas are to be generated.

ATYPICAL CASES

The researcher must distinguish between representative cases and anecdotal cases. Representative cases appear with regularity and encompass the range of behaviours described within a category. The anecdotal case appears infrequently and depicts a small range of events which are atypical of the larger group.

In the case previously cited (Field, 1984) the clients attending the nurse-run clinic who perceived that they had inner control were representative of the modal group of clients attending the clinic. The clients who lacked inner control represented the anecdotal case, their overall behaviour and characteristics were similar to that of the total population but in this one dimension they were atypical of the larger group.

Negative cases are those episodes that clearly refute an emergent theory or proposition. Negative cases are important as they help to clarify additional causal properties which influence the phenomena under study (Denzin, 1978).

ETHNOSCIENCE: BUILDING A TAXONOMY

In ethnoscience data are collected through a series of tape recorded interviews. To ensure adequate depth of understanding a minimum of three interviews is necessary with each informant. The data are transcribed and analyzed between interviews.

Defining the Domain

At the first interview broad questions that clearly define the domain are asked. For example, if the topic is 'difficult patients', broad questions may be, "Have you ever nursed difficult patients?", "What kinds of 'difficult patients' are there?", and "What are the different ways nurses manage 'difficult patients'?" Listen very carefully for lexemes, labels used by the group, in this case the words nurses use to describe the patients. For instance, nurses may describe 'difficult' patients as 'naughty,' 'noisy', or 'bossy', 'attention getting' or as 'a wanderer'. As these types of difficult patients form the basis for each contrast set in the analysis it is important to transcribe and list these lexemes.

Sentence Frames

At the second interview, the attributes of each type of difficult patient are obtained firstly with the use of open-ended questions contrasting two types of patients. For instance, the researcher may ask, "What is the difference between an 'attention-getting' patient and a 'bossy' patient?" Secondly, sentence frames confirm the unique characteristics of each contrast set, and should be used both with the same informant and other informants. Sentence frames are essentially statements which ask the respondent to fill in the blanks. For example:

"A _____ patient _____."
    (type)   (action)

The respondent might complete the sentence as follows:

"A *demanding* patient *rings the bell too often.*"

Card Sorts

Finally, the commonalities between the different types of components are established by the use of diadic and triadic card sorts and the Q-sort. The interviewer writes all the attributes of each component on separate cards and, for the diadic card sort, asks the informant to sort the cards into two piles. When the informant has finished, the researcher asks the informant to name each pile and to describe the differences. For example, the informant may have sorted patient characteristics into two piles, one labelled 'bossy', and the second labelled 'demanding.' The informant is then asked to sort the cards into three piles and to describe and label each pile. This increases the information obtained by the researcher. Some behaviours will remain in the 'bossy' and 'demanding' piles. Behaviours common to both sets of patients may be in the third pile.

In the Q-sort the informant is given the cards to sort into piles. The number of piles is not forced by the researcher but determined by the informant. Again, when the task is finished information concerning the differences and commonalities between each pile is elicited from the informant by the researcher.

Preparation of a Taxonomy

From the segregates and sub-segregates it is possible to sort the categories into a taxonomy. Although there are several styles or methods of presenting the data, the principles are the same. Figure 6.4 shows a taxonomy for difficult patients, indicating the types of difficult patients and some of the characteristics of each that might be identified by nurses. The researcher will now need to search further to determine whether the characteristics are unique to each category and whether further characteristics can be identified related to each classification.

Taxonomies may also be developed that relate to events rather than to people. An example of this would be a taxonomy relating to decision making in childbirth. The first part of the taxonomy may be related to who makes decisions while the second part of the taxonomy identifies the types of decisions that are made by each category of person involved in the process (Figure 6.5). To develop this second taxonomy the researcher

Figure 6.4 Types of Difficult Patients (Fictitious Study)

Example 1:

Difficult Patients											
Naughty				Sick				Non-compliant			
bossy	demanding	manipulating	attention getting	listless	noisy	confused	wandering	unaccepting	unco-operative	stubborn	independent

Example 2:

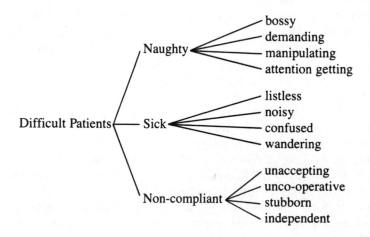

needs to ask structural questions. In this instance information would need to be elicited to determine what types of decisions the informants think they can make in the specified situations. One can ask, 'What are the different kinds of decisions you can make about labour?', 'What are the different ways in which you participated in making decisions?' In asking structural questions one can go from specific to general or general to specific.

Some propositions can be formulated from this taxonomy. These might be related to which participants make decisions during labour and the dimensions in which the various participants hold power to determine the outcome.

The researcher might wish to learn the attributes of a particular category. For example, 'doctor' is a perceptual category, but there are certain structural components that can be identified that further classify the abstract concept. There are types of doctors, with various levels of expertise and experience. A structural question may be, 'What are the different kinds of doctors you encounter in the hospital?' An attribute question, to get more specific responses, could be phrased, 'What is the difference between a general practitioner and a resident?' (or any other paired category). In this manner named categories and their attributes can be developed. The results may be reflected in a table similar to Table 6.1, rather than a diagram as in the two previous examples.

GROUNDED THEORY METHODS

The use of the grounded theory approach enables researchers to develop their own theories relative to the topic they are researching and encourages the use of creative thinking in the process of theory generation. The main processes described by Glaser (1978, p. 17) are identified as theoretical coding, theoretical memos, the generation of core problems, processes and conditions, theoretical sorting, theoretical writing and generating formal theory. While neither Glaser and Strauss (1967) nor Glaser (1978) clearly describe the analytical processes they employ, it would appear that many of the steps used are similar to those described for qualitative research in general. In grounded theory the collection of data is modified as directed by the advancing theory. In similar fashion data collection, coding, categorizing and conceptualization occur almost from the beginning of the study (Stern, 1980). The processes used in analysis do not appear to differ greatly from those used by other qualitative approaches. However, there are some techniques that appear to be peculiar to grounded theory and these will be addressed.

Stern (1980) notes that grounded theory methodology differs from

Figure 6.5 Schema for a Taxonomy of Decision Making in Labour

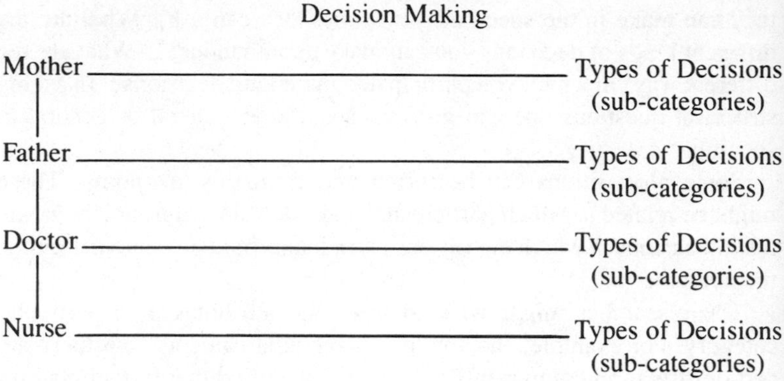

Decision Making

Mother —————————————————	Types of Decisions (sub-categories)
Father —————————————————	Types of Decisions (sub-categories)
Doctor —————————————————	Types of Decisions (sub-categories)
Nurse —————————————————	Types of Decisions (sub-categories)

Table 6.1: Types of Doctors Found in a Labour Ward
According to Mothers' Perceptions

Type	Preparation	Skill	Mother's Reaction
Obstetrician	Specialist	Competent	Confident
General Practitioner	Trained for normal procedures	Competent	Confident
Resident	Qualified doctor becoming a specialist	Somewhat Competent	Ambivalent
Student Interns	Student	Incompetent	Insecure

Source: Field, P.A., Parent Satisfaction with Maternity Care (work in progress).

other methodologies in that the conceptual framework is generated from the data rather than from previous studies. This is, of course, a characteristic that is held in common with many other qualitative approaches. She takes the point further to note that previous studies influence the outcome of the work and in this respect grounded theory probably utilizes other theorists more heavily than do some of the other qualitative approaches.

In grounded theory the researcher attempts to discover the dominant processes in the social setting with the goal of generating hypotheses that will have a generalized applicability. For example, Glaser and Strauss (1967) generated generalized constructs relating to the patient's awareness of dying.

Using this approach, each piece of data is compared with every other piece (the constant comparison) rather than describing only the unit under study (Stern, 1980, p. 21). In this respect grounded theorists do use a more structured form of analysis than do other qualitative researchers. It is suggested that constant comparison be undertaken on a paragraph by paragraph basis but this becomes unrealistic when a large quantity of data is being analyzed. It becomes more practical to undertake initial coding and then compare the findings across interviews.

In all qualitative research the purpose of enquiry is to identify the properties existing in the real world and to gain a fuller understanding of what constitutes reality for the informants in a particular real-life setting. Thus the understanding that emerges from the research is the product of the interaction between the researcher and the phenomena under study. The development of sound grounded theory rests upon a sensitivity to the processes involved in social interaction and human development and on the researcher's ability to both recognize and present them for discussion. This is a difficult task for the beginning researcher and discussion of data and beginning ideas with other researchers should be encouraged when a grounded theory approach is to be employed.

In Turner's (1981) explication of an analytical approach that can be used by those employing grounded theory, nine stages of analysis are identified. A discussion of these stages will be presented.

Category Development and Category Saturation. Category development and saturation are similar processes to those described for qualitative data in general, earlier in this chapter. First labelled categories are developed which are derived from the data. The second stage is category saturation. Examples of identified categories are accumulated until it becomes clear to the researcher those properties and characteristics of the elements which fit into that particular category. The researcher can then identify the criteria for further instances that would fit the specific category.

Glaser and Strauss (1967) write of using 'constant comparison' during this phase of analysis. This means that the data must be examined closely for all instances of phenomena that seem to be similar to determine whether or not there is a fit with the developing category. For example, if one has three interviews with one individual, comparison of data across all three interviews would be required to identify all examples of the category of person, behaviour, or event being labelled or saturated. Comparisons should also be made across interviews provided by different informants. A category is said to be saturated when no new information on the characteristics of the category is forthcoming.

Formulating Abstract Definitions. When the process of establishing and saturating a category has been achieved the researcher must formulate a definition based on the properties inherent in the category. This definition will state the criteria that will be used for putting further instances into the category. The definition acts as a guide for further data gathering and should also stimulate theoretical reflection on the part of the researcher. This is the point where the researcher will contemplate whether the emergent categories bear resemblance to other known work that has been carried out in the field. Glaser and Strauss (1967) insist that the researcher must have a sound knowledge of the general theory in the field of study, but this is for comparative purposes, not for the purpose of forming a framework prior to data analysis.

Using Definitions and Exploiting Categories. It is of critical importance that once initial categories have been formed the researcher continue to search for additional categories. It may also be necessary to reduce categories, making them more specific or more general in nature. As with all data analysis, the search must continue for the negative instance that contradicts or does not fit the criteria that have been identified for the category.

Linking Categories and Testing Links. Links between categories should be noted, described and developed. This is where the initial generation of hypotheses relating to the links occurs. The next stage is the examination of the hypothesized relationships when initial specifications are made regarding the conditions under which the hypotheses hold true.

Connect with Existing Theory. It is during this phase of development that bridges are established to already existing theory. Findings are presented and are then compared with other previously published research.

Test Emerging Relationships. It is important to identify key variables and to test to see if relationships hold within categories and between categories when extreme cases are compared.

DEVELOPING GROUNDED THEORY: AN EXAMPLE

An example from a study of patient care-seeking behaviour will illustrate the process of developing grounded theory.

> I had been in the shopping centre and the kid had been screaming. On the way home in the car he continued to scream. When I took him out I felt ... I felt I just wanted to drop him on his head. I took him upstairs and put him in his crib and closed the door. What sort of a mother am I ... wanting to harm my kid? I remembered a pamphlet on the health workshop. So I called the workshop ... and the nurse came ... I told her about the tantrums ... what could I do? She sat and listened ... she helped me realize I tended to be a perfectionist ... that I needed to relax ... just having her listen made me feel much better.

> Informant: Mother of two year old child.

Categories Generated
Stress situation (overt problem)
Threat to self-concept (covert problem)
Pamphlet as stimulus
Care-Seeking Behaviour: call to health workshop
Role of nurse expected by mother
Actions of nurse perceived by mother
Problem presentation to nurse (overt problem)
Supportive activity: listening
Relief obtained (outcome)

Constant Comparison

The data used in this study were interviews with clients who had received nursing care. After the initial five interviews were analyzed, categories were developed, then the next five interviews were analyzed and the categories compared with those in the first five interviews. In this way saturation of categories was undertaken. By the time the last five interviews were analyzed no new instances of behaviour were identified that did not fit within the previously identified and defined categories. Thus saturation was attained.

Formulating Abstract Definitions

Abstract definitions of the categories were then formulated. One category had the title, 'Definition of a problem by client.' The definition for the category read:

> When a client perceives that a stress situation occurs at a level
> which threatens either self-concept or body-image the client per-
> ceives s/he has a problem and initiates care-seeking behaviour.

Later, a definition of situations in which cumulative stress had occurred
had to be added to an initial definition of a single threat. Also, a category
of behaviour related to trauma as a stimulus to care-seeking had to be
developed. This led to the development of a tentative proposition regarding the precipitating factor in care-seeking behaviour and the agency
selected to provide that care. Thus the categories suggested the potential
for the extension of the enquiry and stimulated the researcher to question
whether one category was related to the next.

Exploitation and Linkage of Categories

Exploitation and linkage of categories led to the identification of three
phases of care-seeking: the pre-active phase, the interactive phase and the
post-active phase. Thus a process of care-seeking was identified. However,
within the interviews was a small group of atypical clients, those who
were referred by other agencies rather than being self-referred. On
examining this group it was noted that their expectations of the nurse and
their satisfaction with the care received differed from that of the self-
referred group. New categories and relationships had to be developed and
new propositions generated relating to this atypical group. This is the
process of exploitation of categories.

In this particular situation it became evident that when expectations
relating to nursing care and perceptions of the care received coincided,
then satisfaction with care resulted.

The linkage between precipitating factors that initiated the care-
seeking behaviour and goals for care became evident as more interviews
were examined. Processes in care-seeking behaviour were identified:

> Having perceived a need for help the individual identifies a prob-
> lem or goal with which to approach a health care agent or agency.

> A dominant problem is selected but the presenting problem may
> only be one symptom of a more complex situation.

> Clients who go through an inter-agency or inter-agent referral
> process may not have an identified problem or goal.

This identification of processes was carried out throughout the three
phases of care-seeking which had been identified.

Connections to Existing Theory

At the time the study was undertaken little research had been published in relation to care-seeking behaviours. However, two propositions related to locus of control were supported by earlier work in the psychological literature. Five hypotheses were generated that identified the behaviours clients engaged in when seeking care. These formed the basis for an emerging theory of care seeking (Field, 1984, p. 252).

From this example it can be seen that much of the process used in developing grounded theory is similar to that of other qualitative research methodologies where participant observation and semi-structured or open-ended interviews are the major data gathering tools.

ISSUES IN QUALITATIVE RESEARCH

In any type of research the researcher must address the issues of objectivity and subjectivity, reliability and validity. The final sections of this chapter will address these issues as they apply to qualitative methodologies.

Subjectivity in Qualitative Research

Qualitative research has been extensively criticized for the subjective nature of the methods. This subjectivity may be derived from firstly the researcher-as-an-instrument, or secondly, from the quality of the evidence or the subjective nature of the research topic.

The Researcher-as-an-Instrument. In qualitative research the amount and quality of the data and the depth of the analysis are dependent upon the ability of the researcher. For example, the information elicited from an interview depends upon the ability of the interviewer to establish rapport and gain trust of the informants, or upon the researcher's interview techniques. In participant observation, the amount of information also depends upon observational skills and the amount of trust established. If trust is not present, then the setting will change when the researcher is present and participants will conceal facts from the researcher. Finally, the depth of the data analysis will depend upon the researcher's sensitivity, perceptivity, informed value judgements, insight and knowledge.

The Quality of the Evidence. Qualitative researchers study people's perceptions and reports or accounts of situations and events. As such, these reports may be 'unreliable', 'biased' and contradict other reports. This problem is known as the 'Rashomon Effect' (Heider, 1983, p. 10) and is the basis of the problems in the law courts when six witnesses may each report a different 'version' of reality. However, in qualitative research such different and discrepant perspectives are considered a part of the context, a part of the problem. For example, a patient's perspective and report of a visit to the doctor may be quite different from the doctor's account of the visit, and both of these reports may differ from an 'objective' observer's report. However, the purpose of qualitative research is not to determine objectively what actually happened (as in the court of law) but rather to objectively report the perceptions of each of the actors in the setting.

VALIDITY AND RELIABILITY IN QUALITATIVE RESEARCH
In any research the ability of individual researchers to demonstrate credibility is critical to the value of the findings. In all research reliability and validity of findings are important. However, the way in which criteria are used for assessing the reliability and validity of a study will vary with the type of research. The questions raised regarding the reliability and validity of a descriptive study may be different from those addressed in a quantitative study because, as previously described, subject selection, data gathering and data analysis are conducted in different ways and for different purposes.

Validity
Validity is the overall concept used to refer to how good an answer a study yields. That is, is the answer provided by the research sound, and does it represent reality? Another concern centers around the question as to whether the internal procedures used in the research distort reality. It is therefore an essential criteria of the research design.

Reliability
Reliability is a constituent element of validity. The concepts of reliability refer to the extent to which random variation may have influenced the study results. It is therefore a central concept in quantitative research in sample selection and instrument development. If a questionnaire is used to collect data it is important to know whether this is reliable, that is, whether one will get the same answers from similar populations using the same questionnaire. If the subjects and the instruments are adequate then there should be consistent results if the study is replicated.

The issue of sample selection and informant representativeness is an area of qualitative research that is frequently questioned by those undertaking empirical research. In a qualitative study the data gathering instrument is frequently the observer or the interviewer. Thus questions of observer bias and observer competency need to be addressed. In the analysis phase the reliability of the coding system must be defended. Some issues relating to sampling, data gathering and analysis will now be addressed.

Le Compte and Goetz (1982) published an excellent analysis of the issues of external and internal validity and reliability comparing concerns in quantitative and qualitative research. The influence of their perspective is evident in the following discussion.

SAMPLING

It is important to select key informants who have knowledge of relevant information. As noted earlier, if one wants to study adolescence, then adolescents must be included as participants in the study. In primitive societies, for example, the perspective of a witch-doctor may be very different than that of the chief. The researcher needs to demonstrate that the informants are credible representatives knowledgeable about the population and who have information on the subject under study.

Data Gathering

Frequently participant observation and unstructured interviews are major methods of data collection. Therefore such questions as observer accuracy, observer focus and observer bias are critical to both validity and reliability.

The researcher's status, the sampling procedures (informant choices), the social context and the conditions under which data are gathered, are all factors which can affect the reliability of the study. The history and maturation of a group, the subject mortality (participant refusal or withdrawal), the effects of the observer on the group and the selection of observations will all influence the validity of a study.

Social Context

The social context under which the data are gathered is an important consideration in establishing reliability and validity of data. Informants will reveal certain information in one context and not in another. Information may be obtained in individual or in group situations. Becker and Geer (1978) suggest that information given in one-to-one situations should be verified with information presented by informants in group situations. In all studies it is useful to verify data with information from several sources. As previously mentioned, Zelditch (1969) and Jick (1979) refer to this as triangulation of data. If one can demonstrate commonality of behaviour across data gathered in different ways the validity of the information is increased.

Homans (1955) outlines six variables that he suggests should be used to evaluate the adequacy of a qualitative study. These are time, place, social circumstance, language, intimacy and consensus. These relate both to the conditions under which the data were gathered and the homogeneity amongst the information gained from individual informants. In discussing the criterion of time Homans notes that the observer must spend sufficient time in the setting to enable adequate contacts to be made and to establish rapport with informants.

The criterion of place refers to the fact that the closer the researcher is to the people he studies the more accurate will be his interpretation of the situation. However, care must be exercised in that the researcher must avoid becoming so much a part of the group that objectivity is lost. The criterion of social circumstance is discussed later and refers to the variety of reported situations in which the behaviour is observed.

The fourth criterion of language maintains that the more familiar the observer is with the language of the participants the greater the accuracy of the interpretations. Similarly, the greater the degree of intimacy that the observer establishes with the informants the more accurate will be the observations until the researcher reaches the stage of 'going native', which again results in in a loss of objectivity. The final criterion is that of consensus, the more the observer confirms the expressed meaning of the informants with other informants the greater the accuracy of the interpretations.

History and Maturation of the Group

When a group is observed over a period of time changes will occur. The extent to which a phenomenon observed when the researcher enters the group is the same at the end of the study, is salient to the research. Whereas the experimental researcher controls the variables, the qualitative researcher studies phenomena in a naturalistic setting which cannot be held constant. Changes that involve development in the social setting itself are considered to be history and are a part of the development of the phenomena. Changes that occur in relation to individuals are considered to be maturation. A change in the organizational structure would thus be history, while promotion of a subject from a follower to a leader position in the social hierarchy would be maturation (Le Compte and Goetz, 1982).

Status of Researcher

The status position of the researcher in the group can be that of an outsider or that of a participant group member. If a female is studying a male secret society she may be an outsider and will not be privy to the information held by the group. Kerewsky-Halpern (1984) reported that in her study of Yugoslavian peasant women she was not privy to some of the healing rituals until she gained the status of 'old woman.' Thus status position can prevent the researcher from obtaining certain information and unless one is aware of this, invalid interpretation of the culture may result. On the other hand, if one becomes totally a part of the group there is a danger of 'going native.' The researcher may then lose the ability to look objectively at what is happening and may develop bias toward the point of view of the group. Whyte, in his study *Street Corner Society* (1955), dealt with this problem by distancing himself from his subjects at regular intervals and discussing his data with university colleagues. This helped him to retain an objective perspective.

Participant Mortality

The ways in which groups change over time as a result of losses in membership pose particular difficulties for ethnographers. In studying the effects of introduction of planned change into a nursing unit, for example, it is of particular importance to account for mortality or attrition. The reason for the withdrawal of informants from the research project or the setting, becomes part of the topic for study. Generally ethnographers assume that the naturalistic approach permits the interchangeability of participants (Le Compte and Goetz, 1982). As attrition is a normal process in most group settings, the task of the researcher becomes one of examining effects.

Observer Variables

It has been suggested that a nurse cannot be an ethnographer by virtue of her nursing training alone (Aamodt, 1982). The wisdom of this statement can be seen when examining the issues of validity and reliability of data collection. An observer needs to be trained in a manner that encourages an objective view of the phenomena under study. Nurses tend to observe patients/clients and interpret their findings in light of their own values. It is probable that they do not always identify their own values and are therefore not aware of their biases (Field, 1980).

Both validity and reliability of observations can be increased through rigorous training of the observer. Every observer makes certain assumptions about the culture being studied. The critical factor is that these assumptions are recognized and declared so they can be considered when reading the research. For example, Glaser and Strauss (1965) become interested in studying dying because both were concerned about the death of a parent who had not been told that they had a terminal illness (Stern *et al.* 1982/4). They started with the bias that non-disclosure of information might not be an appropriate way to help the dying person.

Observer Effects

When a new member is introduced into an interaction it can be anticipated that the nature of that interaction will change. One difficulty in qualitative research is in assessing the effect of the observer on the interaction. One way of decreasing the effect is by spending a period of time in the situation before data collection starts. The observer becomes sensitized to the situation and at the same time the informants have the opportunity to become used to the presence of the observer. This is one reason why a sufficient amount of time needs to be spent in the research setting.

Kratz (1974) and Luker (1978) have both observed that in nurse-client situations when the client knows the researcher is a nurse she becomes one, fused with the care-provider, so that a dyadic rather than a triadic situation exists. This situation may be unique to nursing and the problem of observer bias remains important and one that is difficult to assess. However, up to a point, the longer the study, the less likely that observer bias will have a major role in distorting the data. The longer the observer is present the more her presence is likely to become background to the observed interaction rather than an intrusion into the interaction. Researchers must make a conscientious effort to assess and report their assessment of the effects of the observer in the field setting.

Data Analysis
The standardized protocols necessary for establishing interrater reliability are generally inappropriate for participant observation as they are designed for use with structured observation instruments. It is therefore critical to ascertain whether observers agree with the definitions derived from the data for categorization purposes. This is particularly important when multiple researchers are engaged in a study. In the case of a single investigator it is necessary that categories be clearly described and related to the data. Specific strategies can be used to reduce threats to internal reliability. These include the use of low-inference descriptors, participant reviews of findings and peer examination. If it is necessary to obtain inter-rater reliability the procedures are clearly described elsewhere (Diers, 1979, pp. 240-1; Polit and Hungler, 1978; Miles and Huberman, 1984, p. 63).

Low Inference Descriptors. Low inference descriptors are verbatim accounts of information provided by informants to the researcher. Use of mechanical recording enhances the accuracy of such transcripts. Appropriate low-inference descriptors should be used to substantiate the categories presented in the analysis of the data. Ethnographers who provide readers with rich excerpts from primary fieldnotes are generally considered to be the most credible.

Participant Review of Findings. The use of participant informants to review the analysis ensures that the researcher and the informants are viewing the data consistently. This may not always be possible to do, as showing the analysis to informants may distort further information as there may be an attempt to supply answers that the informant believes the researcher wants to hear.

The use of informants to review the findings may be useful at the conclusion of a study. Even then the researcher and informants may not be in agreement. Kratz (1974) found that the Health Visitors in her study could not understand why she placed particular emphasis on aspects of care which they considered relatively unimportant but which related to the purpose of her study. The researcher must determine whether the objection is related to the validity of the study or whether it is due to a different priority given to the phenomenon by the researcher and the informant.

Peer Examination. Peer examination may involve soliciting colleagues' help in examining the fieldnotes and transcripts to see if they can identify the same categories and structures within the data as the researcher. Such review may also identify trends in the data not discovered by the primary researcher and may open new avenues for exploration. Publication of findings is, of course, always an offering of material for peer review. It is of critical importance that sufficient primary material be included in reports for publication to support the ethnographer's interpretation of data and conclusions.

One problem with internal validity in ethnographic research is that of spurious conclusions. While the researcher may have accounted for the effects of history and maturation, observer impact and selection of informants, spurious relationships among observed phenomena may still present a problem. Idiosyncratic use of constructs by the researcher may result in spurious conclusions being drawn. This is particularly important when researchers wish to make comparisons between groups, as with ethnology.

As previously mentioned, a constant search for negative instances of categories or disconfirming evidence for tentative constructs is critical both in ongoing and terminal analysis of data. Information from inform- ants should be clarified when necessary and alternative possibilities relating to particular phenomena observed. It is critical that the researcher eliminate possible alternative explanations. Presenting an array of the most plausible explanations of causes of a phenomenon rather than delineating one probable cause will also increase the internal validity of a study. The researcher must always think through the way in which each observed factor may have influenced an event. In this way sources of bias or contamination are more likely to be discovered as the study proceeds.

GENERALIZABILITY OF STUDIES

In qualitative or naturalistic research the effects which obstruct a study's comparability or translatability are those which affect the external validity of the study (Wolcott, 1975). Qualitative studies, even with careful description of participants and setting, cannot be replicated exactly. The researcher's purpose is to demonstrate the typicality of a phenomenon observed in a particular situation at a particular period in time. If that phenomenon has been reported in other research it may be cautiously generalized across those situations. It must be remembered that selection of a group may influence the generalizability of an observed phenomenon. Failure to observe this guideline may result in invalid comparisons.

Generalization must therefore be treated with care. Comparisons must take into account the similarities and differences between the groups being compared. The ethnographer's commitment is to an accurate rendition of the life of the participants being studied. Knowledge of eccentric or idiosyncratic groups may be as important as the development of phenomena that can be compared across groups. Remember, generalizability is not the purpose of qualitative research but the purpose is rather to elicit meaning in a given situation and to develop reality-based theory.

FINAL ANALYSIS

After leaving the field the researcher undertakes the final phase of data analysis. At this stage the categories and their properties will be well established and stable. The process now becomes one of ordering data and getting ready to write the final report.

Profitable research is built on a knowledge base, so while a theoretical framework is not pre-determined, sound knowledge of the subject to be studied is essential. The process of finding relationships within data follows the initial process of analysis, that is, the process of category development. This results in the formulation of concepts and hypotheses to accommodate the observed facts. These concepts and hypotheses will in turn give direction to future data collection. The researcher will seek evidence that will either support or disprove the tentative hypotheses (or propositions) that have been formulated.

REFERENCES

Aamodt, A.M. (1982) 'Examining Ethnography for Nurse Researchers', *Western Journal of Nursing Research*, 4(2), 209-21.

Agar, M.H. (1980) *The Professional Stranger: An Informal Introduction to Ethnography*, Academic Press Inc., London.

Babbie, E. (1979) *The Practice of Social Research*, 3rd edn., Wadsworth Publishing Co., Belmont, California.

Becker, H.S. and Geer, B. (1978) 'Participant Observation and Interviewing: A Comparison' in J.G. Manis and B.N. Meltzer (eds.), *Symbolic Interaction: A Reader in Social Psychology*, Allyn and Bacon Inc., Boston, pp. 76-82.

Bogdan, R.C. and Biklen S.K. (1982) *Qualitative Research for Education: An Introduction to Theory and Methods*, Allyn and Bacon, Inc., Boston.

Davis, J. (1972) 'Teachers, Kids and Conflict: Ethnography of Junior High School', in J.P. Spradley and D.W. McCurdy (eds.), *Sociological Methods*, Aldine Publishing Company, Chicago, pp. 103-19.

Denzin, N.K. (1978) *Sociological Methods: A Sourcebook*, 2nd edn., McGraw-Hill, New York.

Diers, D. (1979) *Research in Nursing Practice*, J.B. Lippincott Company, Philadelphia.

Field, P.A. (1980) *Four Nurses' Perspectives of Nursing in a Community Health Setting*, unpublished PhD thesis, University of Alberta, Edmonton.

Field, P.A. (1984) 'Behaviour and Nursing Care' in M. Leininger (ed.), *Care: The Essence of Nursing and Health*, J.B. Slack, New Jersey, pp. 249-62.

Fox, D.J. (1982) *Fundamentals of Research in Nursing* 4th edn., Appleton-Century-Crofts., Norwalk, Connecticut.

Glaser, B. (1978) *Theoretical Sensitivity*, The Sociology Press, Mill Valley, California.

Glaser, B. and Strauss, A. (1965) *Awareness of Dying*, Aldine Publishing Company, Chicago.

Glaser, B. and Strauss, A. (1967) *Discovery of Grounded Theory: Strategies for Qualitative Research*, Aldine Publishing Company, Chicago.

Heider, K. (1983) 'The Rashomon Effect', *Association for Social Anthropology in Oceania Newsletter*, Spring Issue, pp. 10-1.

Homans, G.C. (1955) *The Human Group*, Harcourt Brace, New York.

Jick, T.D. (1979) 'Mixing Qualitative and Quantitative Methods: Triangulation in Action', *Administrative Science Quarterly, 24*, 602-11.

Kerewsky-Halpern, B. (1984) 'Talk, Trust and Touch in Traditional Healing', Paper presented at the University of Alberta, Edmonton, March 24.

Kirk, R.C. (1981) 'Microcomputers in Anthropological Research', *Sociological Methods and Research, 9*(4), 473-92.

Kratz, C.R. (1974) 'Two Methodological Problems', *Nursing Times*, Occasional Papers, *70*, 53-6.

Le Compte, M.D. and Goetz, J.P. (1982) 'Problems of Reliability and Validity in Ethnographic Research', *Review of Educational Research, 52*(1), 31-60.

Lofland, J. (1971) *Analyzing Social Settings: A Guide to Qualitative Observation and Analysis* Wadsworth Publishing Co. Inc., Belmont, California.

Luker, K.A. (1978) 'Goal Attainment: A Possible Model for Assessing the Role of the Health Visitor', *Nursing Times*, Occasional Papers, *74*, 1257-9.

Miles, M.B. and Huberman, A.M. (1984) *Qualitative Data Analysis: A Sourcebook of New Methods*, Sage Publications, Inc., Beverly Hills, California.

124   *The Process of Analyzing Data*

Morse, J.M. and Doan, H. (1984) 'Becoming a Woman: Adolescents' Responses to Menarche', Paper presented to the Society for Applied Anthropology, Toronto, Ontario.

Murdock, G. (1971) *Outline of Cultural Materials*, Human Relation Area Files Press, New Haven, Connecticut.

Podolefsky, A. and McCarty, C. (1983) 'Topical Sorting: A Technique for Computer Assisted Qualitative Data Analysis', *American Anthropologist, 85*(4), 886-90.

Polit, D. and Hungler, B. (1978) *Nursing Research: Principles and Methods*, J.B. Lippincott Company, New York.

Rogoff, B. (1978) 'Spot Observation: An Introduction and Examination', *Institute for Comparative Human Development, 2*(2), 21-6.

Spradley, J.P. (1980) *Participant Observation*, Holt, Rinehart and Winston, New York.

Sproull, L.E. and Sproull, R.F. (1982) 'Managing and Analyzing Behavioral Records: Explanations in Non-numeric Data Analysis', *Human Organization, 41*(4), 283-90.

Stern, P.N. (1980) 'Grounded Theory Methodology: Its Uses and Processes', *Image, 12*(11), 20-3.

Stern, P.N., Allen, L.M. and Moxley, P.A. (1984) 'Qualitative Research: The Nurse as Grounded Theorist', *Health Care for Women International*, 5, 371-385 (Original work published 1982).

Turner, B. (1981) 'Some Practical Aspects of Qualitative Data Analysis: One Way of Organizing the Cognitive Processes Associated with the Generation of Grounded Theory', *Quality and Quantity, 15*, 225-47.

Whyte, W.F. (1955) *Street Corner Society*, 2nd edn., University of Chicago Press, Chicago.

Wolcott, H. (1975) 'Criteria for an Ethnographic Approach to Research in Schools', *Human Organization, 34*(2), 111-28.

Zelditch, M. Jr. (1969) 'Some Methodological Problems of Field Studies' in B.J. McCall and J.L. Simmons (eds.), *Issues in Participant Observation: A Text and Reader*, Addison-Wesley Publishing Company, Menlo Park, California, pp. 5-19.

Chapter Seven

REPORTING QUALITATIVE RESEARCH

The main purpose of conducting research is to disseminate the research findings to others. Through publication the findings are available to teachers for the promotion of understanding, for students to increase knowledge, for researchers to build on and for clinicians to use. Without publication the research process becomes a futile endeavour. Reward only comes when findings are shared or implemented.

While many of the points mentioned here may be used in writing any written report, qualitative research requires a different writing style. In this chapter, common problems that occur in writing, methods to facilitate writing and the preparation of a qualitative research report will be discussed.

PITFALLS IN WRITING

Writers Block

The major difficulty in writing is 'getting started'. Frequently, more time is wasted sharpening pencils, sighing at the desk, doodling and discarding 'false starts' than is spent actually writing!

The first reason for this difficulty is that very often, the writer has not clearly thought through exactly what is to be written. The ideas about the content of the article have not been clearly identified and planned.

This preliminary planning may be done as a thinking task while walking or jogging, or over a glass of wine one evening. If the ideas cannot be recited to one's self then find a friend who will listen to an explanation of the proposed article. A tape recorder (which doesn't answer back) may be substituted for the friend. This has the advantage that the ideas are preserved on tape and can be retrieved. This process of making the ideas clear to another, also clarifies and assists with the articulation of the ideas essential for writing.

The second reason for the writer's block is the lack of an outline. The pen is slower than the brain and can only write one idea at a time. An outline ensures an orderly, logical progression through either a report or an article and ensures that ideas will not be omitted or lost. Many people write by speaking aloud or by thinking of each word as it is written, thus preventing the mind from wandering and keeping attention focused on the task at hand.

Writing is sometimes inhibited for lack of a first word. If this is the case, write 'The' on the page. Many documents begin with this word and at least the article will be started!

Forgetting a word can be frustrating to the writing process. If this happens do not stop writing, leave a space and continue. The word may be recalled later, or a substitute found in a dictionary of synonyms and antonyms or a word list.

If starting is still a problem, then write the section that is best understood first. There are no rules that dictate that an article must be written in order from the introduction to the conclusion. With an outline it is possible to write the article in sections, according to the writer's mood and time available. The section on methods is an easy place to start writing, as the researcher is most familiar with that material and the section is usually relatively structured. It is wise to write the introduction last, before the abstract, as the writer then fully comprehends the material to which the reader is to be introduced.

The Language of Research

After reading numerous articles and sitting in research courses, the language of research becomes ingrained. But until this language becomes reflexive, speaking 'research-ese' is difficult.

A research article is not the place for emotive words, for colloquialisms, or for unnecessary adjectives. Research reports are crisp and 'dry,' with relatively short sentences.

A list of commonly used words that are not used in research reports and their 'approved' equivalents are presented in Table 7.1. The list is not complete, and can be expanded (unfortunately).

Analyzing and Synthesizing

In research courses students frequently learn the art of critiquing articles. Unfortunately the art of discussing and reviewing many articles is less frequently taught. Yet, in a literature review and discussion section, it is necessary to refer to multiple articles in summary form.

When the student does not analyze the content of articles by searching for common themes or concepts, the literature review is likely to be lengthy. The tendency is to summarize each research report in a separate paragraph without making the appropriate linkages within the literature that has been reviewed. It is critical to analyze and synthesize findings from a variety of studies and report them succinctly.

One method is to approach the literature using concepts or variables to explain and classify previous research. Thus, rather than addressing

Table 7.1 Learning Research Language

Poor Words	Research Equivalent
looking at the...	examining the...
say that...	state
point out...	indicate that...
seems that...	implies that...
the author feels that...	the author suggests that...
the study says...	the researcher demonstrates...
the research found...	it was found that...
shows	portrays... illustrates... demonstrates...
carried out...	conducted...
arbitrary...	(no equivalent; nothing is arbitrary in research)

individual research, the main approaches or findings of several studies
are explained and lists of appropriate citations appear after each point.
This permits the reader to acquire a broad overview of the background
information. However, research which is closest to the research question
should be individually addressed and critiqued.

Editing

An important facilitator to the writing process is the realization that the
writing may be rewritten and edited. The critical thing is to get the ideas
onto paper. The first draft of a report or an article does not have to be
word-perfect with flowing sentences. The writing style can be corrected
by editing the original draft, or if necessary the original document may be
rewritten to expand areas which are 'not clear' or to correct disjointed
paragraphs. Editing is a relatively easy task once the initial ideas have
been written, but until the first draft is completed, this step cannot begin.

PREPARING THE QUALITATIVE REPORT

The process of dissemination of information may entail one or more
stages. A one stage process is the writing of an article for publication
directly from the results. Another example would be the preparation of a
report for a granting body and the publication of that same report as a
monograph. An example of a multi-phase dissemination process is the
preparation of a report or thesis and the subsequent publication of the
report or thesis as one or more journal articles. This section will describe
the process of the preparation of the finished report, monograph or article
from the data analysis stage of the project.

Defining the Audience

Before beginning to write decide what to say and to whom it is to be said.
This may involve considerable reflection. If the report is for a lay funding
body, or a lay audience, decide how the report will best meet their needs
and how the style of writing and the jargon in the report will affect their
comprehension and eventually facilitate or impede the impact of the
report. For example, is the article or report to influence staff nurses,
physicians or patients? Each of these groups has its own distinctive style
and preparing a report for physicians would be considered 'dry', boring
and incomprehensible to patients or a report written for patients, would
be considered simplistic by physicians.

Identifying the Journal

If writing an article, identify suitable journals for publication at this time.
Again, examine the fit of the research with the general subject matter and

the type of research methods usually published by that journal. For instance, some journals will publish any 'health related' article including nursing articles, while other journals prefer articles that are written especially for nurses. Some journals may publish quantitative research methods, while others (such as *Qualitative Sociology*) solicit only qualitative articles, and yet other journals publish both qualitative and quantitative research.

Obtain a copy of the 'instructions for authors' from a recent copy of the journal. This may be printed in a special section of the journal (frequently inside the back cover, or on the masthead of the journal). More detailed instructions may be obtained by writing directly to the editor. Consulting the writing instructions at this time will prevent major editing in later drafts to correct format or to comply with instructions on length.

The Query Letter
Most instruction manuals on writing articles suggest that the author, at this stage, forward the editor a letter of intent for submission, known as a query letter. This letter consists of a *brief* outline of the article (very brief), the approximate length of the article, a statement on why the researcher is qualified to write the article and the expected date of submission. The purpose of the letter is to notify the editor of the potential submission so that forthcoming issues may be planned and to allow the editor an opportunity to give the author some feedback and guidance. For example, if the editor has two or three articles on that topic, the answer may be that, at present, the editor is not interested in the article. Thus the query letter is intended to save the author work. As Swanson and McCloskey (1982) noted, some editors felt that query letters made additional work for their staff. If the article is to be sent for review, a query letter does not facilitate planning.

Organizing the Data
At the writing stage the data will have been analyzed and the results will have been examined. It is still necessary to organize these data into tables and figures and to determine what to include in the article, what to summarize in the text and what to omit. Until this step has been completed, it is not possible to begin outlining the article.

Qualitative research articles may be clearer if the results are summarized in a table. For instance, in their study on the adolescent's response to menarche, Morse and Doan (1984) list all the affective responses reported by the 7th and 8th grade girls, before describing and illustrating each of these feelings with representative quotations from the adolescents' responses. This enables the reader to obtain a more comprehensive perspective on the ranges and types of feelings the girls reported about their first menstruation before detailed descriptions are presented.

Preparing the Outline

An outline provides guidance for writing. It ensures that all necessary content is included, that the writer stays 'on track' and does not wander from the topic or include extraneous material. It also means that, if the writer has a block and has trouble starting to write the introduction, this section may be left and other sections completed first. As the introduction is frequently the most difficult section of an article to write, it may be easier to write if it is written last.

There are many types of outlines, some more detailed than others. The point-form outline may consist of key words and prompts, while the sentence-outline may consist of whole sentences or phrases which may be used in the final document. An example of a point-form outline is shown in Figure 7.1

In the outline indicate where tables and figures will be discussed in the article; if anecdotes or quotations from the data are to be used, prepare these so they may be easily located and included in the text.

Styles of Writing

Over the years protocols for writing quantitative research have been refined so that there are definite rules for writing an article. The writer, for example, follows the format of: introduction, statement of the problem, definition of terms, literature review, hypotheses, methods (setting, subjects, instruments, data collection), data analysis, results, discussion, implications for nursing and implications for further research.

Qualitative research, on the other hand, may or may not follow this outline depending on the type of method used. For example, as phenomenology focuses on the *meaning* of phenomena, phenomenological writing does not use this style. Even the research question may not be stated in question form (Van Manen, 1984). On the other hand, it may be appropriate to follow the format if ethnoscience is being used.

The style of qualitative writing depends on the purpose of the article and the audience. As previously mentioned, if the article is being written for a lay audience, let the people in the study tell their own story. In the following example, the barriers to seeking health care were analyzed (Morse, 1983, p. 78). One of the categories was labelled 'sick enough for the doctor'.

> A common statement given by people who did not go to the doctor was that their complaints were not serious enough to *bother the doctor*. There was a belief that doctors should not have their time

Figure 7.1 Example of Point-Form Outline

Title: Lay Perceptions of Illness Causation

I.   Introduction
    A.   Justification of study
        1.   Study question

II.   Literature Review

III.   Method
    A.   Explanation of qualitative approach
    B.   Selection of informants
    C.   Interview
        1.   Tape recording
        2.   Initial open-ended questions
        3.   Subsequent questions
    D.   Data Analysis
        1.   Transcription
        2.   Coding
        3.   Identification of Domain

IV.   Results
    A.   Overview of results (Table 1 here)
        1.   Illness is genetically acquired
        2.   Illness as a result of early childhood
            experiences
        3.   External control of illness
        4.   Psychological cause of illness
        5.   Germ theory of disease
        6.   Illness and eating
            i.   overeating
            ii.   insufficient food
            iii.   junk food
            iv.   'poisonous food'
            v.   alcohol

V.   Discussion
    A.   Evidence of lay comprehension
    B.   Beliefs of illness causation and health
        behaviors
    C.   Comparison of lay theories of illness with
        professional theories of illness
    D.   Implications for health care workers
    E.   Conclusions

'taken up' for minor problems, but only be consulted when it was *absolutely necessary.*

> ...she hasn't been down to the doctor for years. They have enough to do, she figures. A lot of people even go to the doctor with a sore thumb, but she doesn't bother with doctors.

> Then, if I can't do anything for myself, I will go to the doctor ... because I don't want to monopolize his time unless it is absolutely necessary.

This attitude was also applied to requests for housecalls. One woman with arthritis said:

> I thought I had no right to ask him to come, because there are lots of people that needed his services first, and I don't ... I hesitated to do it (call him).

If the article or report is for a peer group, or a scholarly journal, present the analysis descriptively using quotes to illustrate a concept. In a study on childbirth in Fiji, Morse (1984, p. 9) wrote of the Fiji-Indian Moslem women:

> The lifestyle of the pregnant woman continues without compromise for the pregnancy, which is not disclosed (even to the closest relatives) until the increasing abdominal size (at five or six months) can no longer be concealed. No special concessions are made regarding the pregnant woman's work role. If she is married to a cane farmer, she continues her work in the fields. She receives no nutritional supplementation, and as she has the lowest status in the household, she is served food last. Although it is not required that pregnant women observe a fast, a Moslem woman explained that ''One gets more care from God if this (a fast) was observed — and the baby would be safer''.

Protecting Participants' Identity

When negotiating for permission to enter a setting, to observe or to interview an informant, it is usual practice to promise the organization that they will not be identified in the final report. Therefore, in the report the institution is not named, but rather described in generalities such as: 'a two-hundred-bed gerontological unit situated in the midlands', or 'a general hospital of approximately 1400 beds situated in a large urban center in eastern Canada.' Often, the setting is indirectly disclosed if in the report long lists of names and positions of administrators are listed in the acknowledgements section. Should total concealment be requested, then the researcher must remind the agency that public acknowledgements will be forfeited at all levels.

Concealing the identities of the informants is often a little more difficult. Researchers frequently leave identifiers in the results which may pinpoint the informant. For instance, it is easy to write: 'a 24-year-old staff nurse, with two years of experience noted that...' and it does not need a detective to trace down the informant. Take care when reporting demographic identifiers such as age, sex, and cultural group affiliations. When sample sizes are small and the researcher recognizes that participants may be identified by their ages, it is acceptable to systematically alter all ages in the report by increasing or decreasing the ages by a constant, such as two years for elderly adults. This systematic bias is not large enough to move the elderly out of their developmental age range, but does mean that someone familiar with the respondent will not be able to identify verbatim quotes. Remember to note in the preface, or in a footnote, that the names and other identifiers have been changed to protect the participants' identities. Finally, if there is any doubt, give the article or report to the informant to read and approve prior to distribution.

Unwelcome Results

In the course of qualitative research, it is possible that some data will be essential to the study, which the host organization will not 'like'. For example, observations of nurse-patient interactions may elicit some examples of non-therapeutic behaviour on the part of the nurses or observations that reveal less-than-ideal care. Clearly, including these aspects in the report will not endear the researcher to the host organization. They may also not be inclined to host subsequent researchers in their clinical areas, yet omitting these aspects clearly biases the data. The researcher is in a dilemma between presenting accurate findings and offending the host organization. The bind may be severe enough to inhibit writing. What should the researcher do?

First of all, make sure all the findings included are really essential to the report. If they are not necessary and more is to be lost than gained by including this material, then leave it out.

Secondly, write the report describing the situation as it really is, accurately presenting all information. Then, when the report is completed ask a trusted colleague to 'censor' it, by surveying it for all potentially offensive material. Frequently when the findings are presented within context, the 'inflammatory' data are not as inflammatory as at first thought. The concern over possible ramifications may be worse in the imagination of the researcher than in the actual document. However, if parts of the document are controversial it is simple to modify these sections after the initial writing is complete. Next there is always the inclusive royal 'we'. Present the results so that you are included with the participants: 'We, as nurses, need to be aware...' This technique removes most of the threat and the accusations of the negative results and enables the report to be more easily accepted and used constructively by the organization.

Typing

In qualitative research reports there are several conventions not found in quantitative reports. When reporting quotations from the data to illustrate concepts it is permissable to edit these quotes. If, for example, only a part of the quotation is needed, indicate that some of the text has been removed by placing three dots in the text. Thus: 'John — he is coming home soon — thinks nurses don't think for themselves' may be edited to 'John ... thinks nurses don't think for themselves'.

Explanations to illustrate or explain points, or comments made by the researcher, may be inserted into the quotation with square brackets:

> John [husband] ... thinks nurses don't think for themselves! [In what way?] Well — they make you wait when the doctor's not around, and don't even ask you what's wrong!

Alternatively, if the researcher's comments are lengthy, both the participants and the researcher's comments are set in separate blocks with the speaker identified at the beginning:

> Ann: "John [husband] ... thinks nurses don't think for themselves!"
>
> Researcher: "In what way?"
>
> Ann: "Well — they make you wait even when the doctor's not around, and don't even ask you what's wrong!"

Note that the pauses are noted with dashes, and although some redundancies are removed from the quote, enough expression is left to maintain the speaker's character. If a grammatical error is in the quotation, this should be left in, but acknowledged with a 'sic'.

When preparing an article, it makes the typing process easier if the typist is given a copy of the journal's format instructions to follow. This helps to prevent costly errors. Finally, when sending an article for publication, keep a copy in the files. Many publishers do not return articles if they are rejected.

Presenting Suggestions for Further Study

A normal part of any project is a section at the end in which the researcher makes recommendations for further research. This is also a part of qualitative research reports. However, if the purpose of qualitative research was to develop hypotheses, it is appropriate to list these here. The list may be extensive. Fotopoulos, Dintruff, Costello and Cook (1981), in their article on adaptation to breast cancer, listed 12 hypotheses, plus nine issues to be addressed in future research. Thus the research process is never finished or closed and this is particularly the case with qualitative research:

> I have not succeeded in answering my problem. The answers I have found only serve to raise a whole new set of new questions. In some ways I feel I am as confused as ever, but I believe I am confused at a higher level and about more important things.
>
> Anonymous

REFERENCES

Fotopoulos, S.S., Dintruff, D.L., Costello, K.B. and Cook, M.R. (1981) 'Adaptation to Breast Cancer: Attributional Issues' in P.A. Ahmed (ed.), *Living and Dying With Cancer*, H. Sevier, New York, pp. 131-152.

Morse, J.M. (1983) *Perceptions of Health and Illness in Inner City Edmonton*, unpublished project report, Boyle McCauley Health Centre, Edmonton, Alberta.

Morse, J.M. (1984) 'Cultural Variation in the Behavioral Response to Parturition: Childbirth in Fiji', unpublished paper presented to the Canadian Association for Medical Anthropology, Quebec.

Morse, J.M. and Doan, H. (1984) 'Becoming A Woman: The Adolescent's Response to Menarche', unpublished paper presented to the Society for Applied Anthropology, Toronto

Swanson, E. and McCloskey, J.C. (1982) 'The Manuscript Review Process of Nursing Journals', *Image*, *14*(3), 72-6.

Van Manen, M. (1984) 'Practicing Phenomenological Writing', *Phenomenology + Pedagogy*, *2*(1), 36-9.

GLOSSARY

Coding
The process of identifying persistent words, phrases, themes or concepts within the data so that the underlying patterns can be identified and analyzed.

Concept
A phenomenon which has been identified by common recognition or by formal definition.

Conceptual Framework
A theoretical model developed to show relationships between constructs. It is often used in qualitative research for the identification of variables.

Construct
A term comprised of several concepts which is, therefore, more encompassing and more abstract than a single concept.

Deduction
The process of inferring future outcome from previous research or prior theoretical speculation.

Deductive Theory
Variables, concepts, constructs and hypotheses are derived from previous research and relationships are tested during the research process. Theory is used to guide data collection and analysis.

Emic
The study and analysis of a setting or behaviour interpreted from the author's perspective. Thus, cultural explanations and patterns are inductively 'discovered' within the cultural context rather than analyzed from the researcher's perspective or on a prior framework or theory.

Etic
The study and analysis of behaviour interpreted from the perspective of the observer. Etic analysis of events and patterns permit cross-cultural generalizations to be made.

Generalizability
Generalizability is the extent to which the findings of the research may be applied to other situations or settings.

Grounded Theory
A primarily inductive approach to theory development in which emerging hypotheses are tested deductively and subsequent theory and data collection modified until the optimal fit between the data and theory has been obtained.

Hypothesis
A proposition or a predicted relationship between variables.

Inductive Theory
Variables, concepts, constructs and hypotheses are derived from relationships observed during the process of coding the data. Thus, theory is constructed to explain the observed relationships as they emerge from the data.

Informants
Members of the social or cultural group in the research context who provide information and assistance with the interpretation of the setting. A key informant is the informant from whom the majority of information is obtained. Secondary informants are used by the researcher to confirm or refute the information (provided by the key informant) or to widen the data base as theory is developed or to search for negative cases.

Lexeme
A local name, or a label or slang term, used to describe or refer to characteristics of a person, object, place or thing.

Paradigm
A collection of logically connected concepts and propositions that provides a theoretical perspective or orientation that frequently guides research approaches towards a topic.

Participant
An individual who provides the researcher with information relevant to the study or who consents to be observed during the course of the research. Informants are also participants and the two terms may be used interchangeably. A participant is a subject in the quantitative study.

Phenomenology
Phenomenology is a philosophy and a research approach that focuses on the meaning of the 'lived experience'. The intention is to examine and describe phenomena as they appear in the lived experience of the individual. Thus human experience is inductively derived and described with the purpose of discovering the essence of meaning.

Qualitative Methods
Inductive, holistic, emic, subjective, and process-oriented research methods used to understand, interpret, describe and develop theory pertaining to a phenomenon or a setting.

Quantitative Methods
Positivistic, deductive, particularistic, objective research methods primarily designed to test hypotheses or establish relationships.

Reliability
The measure of the extent to which random variation may have influenced the stability and consistency of the results.

Respondent
A person who voluntarily consents to complete a questionnaire or survey.

Subject
A participant in a research project usually used by the researcher to test hypotheses.

Taxonomy
A classification system which organizes components into sub-categories (or sub-segregates) according to common characteristics.

Theory
The researcher's perception of reality in which concepts are identified, relationships are proposed and predictions are made or results prescribed.

Triangulation
The use of multiple methods to study the same phenomenon.

Validity
In qualitative research, validity refers to the extent to which the research findings represent reality.

Variables
The measurable characteristics of a concept and consist of logical groupings of attributes.

BIBLIOGRAPHY

This bibliography is divided into sections and is intended to supplement the references provided at the end of each chapter. The first section contains references of general interest to those engaged in qualitative research. This is followed by listings of books and articles related to theory development, qualitative approaches, methods of data collection, ethical considerations and data analysis. The second half of the bibliography provides examples of research studies in nursing and related health fields that have used specific qualitative approaches or data gathering methods.

General References
These general references are drawn from research writings that are based on both the anthropological and sociological traditions of qualitative research. They provide an overview of methods and approaches used by qualitative researchers.

Agar, M. *The Professional Stranger: An Informal Introduction to Ethnography* (Academic Press, New York, 1980)

Babbie, E. *The Practice of Social Research*, 3rd edn. (Wadsworth Publishing Company Inc., Belmont, California, 1983)

Beteille, A. 'The Dangers of Research Methodology', *International Social Science Journal*, vol. 28 (1976), pp. 195-7

Bogdan, R.C. and Biklen, S.K. *Qualitative Research for Education: An Introduction to Theory and Methods* (Allyn and Bacon, Toronto, 1982)

Bogdan, R. and Taylor, S.J. *Introduction to Qualitative Research Methods: A Phenomenological Approach to the Social Sciences* (John Wiley and Sons, New York, 1975)

Borzak, L. (ed.) *Field Study: A Sourcebook for Experimental Learning* (Sage Publications Ltd., Beverly Hills, California, 1981)

Bowen, E.S. *Return to Laughter* (Doubleday Inc., New York, 1964)

Bruyn, S.R. *The Human Perspective in Sociology* (Prentice Hall, Englewood Cliffs, New Jersey, 1966)

Cook, T.D. and Reichardt, C.S. *Qualitative Methods in Evaluation Research* (Sage Publications, Beverly Hills, California, 1979)

Deising, P. *Patterns of Discovery in the Social Sciences* (Aldine Publications, New York, 1971)

Denzin, N.K. *The Research Act: A Theoretical Introduction to Sociological Methods* (Aldine Publications, New York, 1973)

———— *Sociological Methods: A Sourcebook*, 2nd edn (McGraw-Hill, New York, 1978)

Diers, D. *Research in Nursing Practice* (J.B. Lippincott, Philadelphia, 1979)

Doan, H. and Morse, J. 'Roadblocks for Researching Menstruation', *Health Care for Women International* (in press)

Dobbert, M.C. *Ethnographic Research* (Praeger Special Studies, Praeger Publishers, New York, 1982)

Douglas, J. *Investigative Social Research* (Sage Publications, Beverly Hills, California, 1976)

Feyerabend, P. *Against Method* (Varo, London, 1978)

Filstead, W.J. *Qualitative Methodology: Firsthand Involvement with the Social World* (Rand McNally College Publishing Company, Chicago, 1970)

Fox, D.J. *Fundamentals of Research in Nursing*, 4th edn (Appleton-Century-Crofts, Norwalk, New Jersey, 1982)

Freilich, M. *Natives at Work: Anthropologists in the Field* (John Wiley and Sons, New York, 1977)

Geertz, C. *The Interpretation of Cultures* (Basic Books Inc., New York, 1973)

Golde, E. (ed.) *Women in the Field: Anthropological Experiences* (Aldine Publishing Company, Chicago, 1970)

Harris, M. *The Rise of Anthropological Theory* (Thomas Y. Crowell, New York, 1968)

Henry, F. and Saberwal, S. *Stress and Responses in Fieldwork* (Holt, Rinehart and Winston, New York, 1969)

Kratz, C.R. 'Two Methodological Problems', *Nursing Times*, Occasional papers, vol. 70 (1974), pp. 53-6

Manis, J.G. and Meltzer, B.N. *Symbolic Interaction* (Allyn and Bacon, Boston, 1978)

McHugh, P., Raffel, S., Foss, D.C. and Blum, A.F. *The Beginning of Social Inquiry* (Routledge and Kegan Paul, London, 1974)

Mead, M. 'Toward a Human Science', *Science*, vol. 191, pp. 903-9

Morse, J. *Methodology and the Minor Matter of Sampling*, unpublished manuscript, University of Alberta, Edmonton

Murdock, G. *Outline of Cultural Materials* (Human Relation Area Files Press, New Haven, Connecticut, 1971)

Naroll, R. and Cohen, R. *A Handbook of Method in Cultural Anthropology* (Columbia University Press, New York, 1970)

Osborne, O.H. (1977) 'Emic-Etic Issues in Nursing Research: An Analysis of Three Studies' in M.V. Batey (ed.), *Communicating Nursing Research: Research in the Bicentennial Year*, vol. 9 (Western Interstate Commission for Higher Education, Boulder Colorado), pp. 373-81

Pelto, P.J. and Pelto, G.H. *Anthropological Research: The Structure of Inquiry* (Cambridge University Press, Cambridge, 1978)

Polit, D. and Hungler, B. *Nursing Research Principles and Methods* (J.B. Lippincott Company, New York, 1978)

Schartz, H. and Jacobs, J. *Qualitative Sociology: A Method to the Madness* (Free Press, New York, 1979)

Smith, R.B. and Manning, P.K. (eds.) *Qualitative Methods: Volume II of Handbook of Social Science Methods* (Ballinger Publishing Company, Cambridge, Massachusetts, 1982)

Tomovic, V.A. *Definitions in Sociology* (Diliton Publications, St. Catharines, Ontario, 1979)

Van Maanen, J. *Qualitative Methodology* (Sage Publications, Beverly Hills, California, 1983)

Wax, R. *Doing Fieldwork: Warnings and Advice* (University of Chicago Press, Chicago, 1971)

Webb, E.J., Campbell, D.J., Schwartz, R.D. and Sechrest, L. *Unobtrusive Measures: Nonreactive Research in the Social Sciences* (Rand McNally College Publishing Co., Chicago, 1966)

Whyte, W.F. *Street Corner Society*, 2nd edn (University of Chicago Press, Chicago, 1955)

Zelditch, M. Jr. 'Some Methodological Problems of Field Studies' in B.J. McCall and J.L. Simmons (eds.), *Issues in Participant Observation: A Text and Reader* (Addison-Wesley Publishing Company, Menlo Park, California, 1969), pp. 5-19

Theory Development and the Qualitative Paradigm
These references present some critical views on theory development, levels of theory and appropriate methodologies for theory development. Issues related to use of the qualitative and quantitative paradigms are explored by some authors.

Dickoff, J. and James, P. 'Researching Research's Role in Theory Development', *Nursing Research*, vol. 17 (1968), pp. 197-203

Diers, D. *Research in Nursing Practice* (J.B. Lippincott, Philadelphia, 1979)

Downs, F.S. 'It's A Great Idea — But It Won't Work', *Nursing Research*, vol. 31, no. 1 (1982), p. 4

Glaser, B.G. and Strauss, A.L. 'The Purpose and Credibility of Qualitative Research', *Nursing Research*, vol. 15, no. 1 (1966), pp. 56-61

Kuhn, T.S. *The Structure of Scientific Revolutions* (University of Chicago Press, Chicago, 1962)

Levi-Strauss, C. *Structural Anthropology* (Basic Books Inc., New York, 1963)

Miles, M.B. 'Qualitative Data as an Attractive Nuisance', *Administrative Science Quarterly*, vol. 24 (1979), pp. 590-601

Mishler, E. 'Meaning in Context: Is There Any Other Kind?', *Harvard Educational Review*, vol. 49 (1979), pp. 1-19

Munhall, P.L. 'Methodological Fallacies: A Critical Self-Appraisal', *Advances in Nursing Science*, vol. 5, no. 4 (1983), pp. 41-9

Smith, J.K. 'Quantitative Versus Qualitative Research: An Attempt to Clarify the Issue', *Educational Research*, vol. 12, no. 3 (1983), pp. 6-13

Swanson, J.M. and Chenitz, W.C. 'Why Qualitative Research in Nursing?', *Nursing Outlook*, vol. 30 (1982), pp. 241-5

Trend, M.G. 'On the Reconciliation of Qualitative and Quantitative Analyses: A Case Study', *Human Organization*, vol. 37 (1978), pp. 345-54

Watson, J. 'Nursing's Scientific Quest', *Nursing Outlook*, vol. 29 (1981), pp. 413-6

General Issues in Theory Development and Validity

This section presents a series of articles which address some issues relating to conflicting views of theory and problems of theory development. These issues are addressed within the framework of the authors' own area of research.

Bohannon, L. 'Shakespeare in the Bush', *Natural History*, vol. 75, no. 7 (1966), pp. 28-33

Cicourel, A.V. (1964) *Method and Measurement in Sociology* (Free Press, New York)

Englehardt, H.T. 'The Diseases of Masturbation: Values and the Concept of Disease' in J.W. Leavitt and R.L. Nunbes (eds.), *Sickness and Health in America: Readings in the History of Medicine and Public Health* (University of Wisconsin Press, Madison, 1978), pp. 15-23

Geertz, C. 'From the Native's Point of View: On the Nature of Anthropological Understanding' in P. Rabinow and W.M. Sullivan (eds.), *Interpretative Social Science: A Reader* (University of California Press, Berkeley, 1979), pp. 225-41

Heider, K. 'The Rashomon Effect', *Association for Social Anthropology in Oceania Newsletter*, Spring Issue (1983), pp. 10-1

Homans, G.C. *The Human Group* (Harcourt Brace, New York, 1955)

Jewell, D.P. 'A Case of a "Psychotic" Navaho Indian Male' in N. Klein (ed.), *Culture, Curers and Contagion* (Chandler and Sharp Publishers Inc., Navato, California, 1979), pp. 155-65

Munhall, P.L. 'Methodological Fallacies: A Critical Self-Appraisal', *Advances in Nursing Science*, vol. 5, no. 4 (1983), pp. 41-9

Tesh, S. 'Disease Causality and Politics', *Journal of Health, Politics, Policy and Care*, vol. 6, no. 3 (1981), pp. 369-90

Zborowski, M. 'Cultural Components in Responses to Pain', *Journal of Social Issues*, vol. 8 (1952), pp. 16-20

Ethical Issues in Qualitative Research

The authors presented in this section explore some of the issues and dilemmas faced by the qualitative researcher when undertaking fieldwork. The problems of coercion, informed consent and basic ethical principles for conducting fieldwork are included.

Abdellah, F.G. 'Approaches to Protecting the Rights of Human Subjects', *Nursing Research*, vol. 16, no. 4 (1967), p. 317

Annas, G.J., Glantz, L.H., and Katz, B.F. *Informed Consent to Human Experimentation: The Subject's Dilemma* (Ballinger Publishing Company, Cambridge, Massachusetts, 1977)

Antle-May, K. 'The Nurse as Researcher: Impediment to Informed Consent?', *Nursing Outlook*, vol. 27, no. 1 (1979), p. 38

Armiger, C.R. 'Ethics of Nursing Research', *Nursing Research*, vol. 26, no. 5 (1977), p. 333

Cassell, J. 'Ethical Principles for Conducting Fieldwork', *American Anthropologist*, vol. 82 (1980), pp. 28-41

Estroff, S.E. and Churchill, L.R. 'Comment 1' (Ethical Dilemmas), *Anthropology Newsletter*, vol. 25, no. 7 (1984), p. 15

'Proposed Code of Ethics Would Supercede Principles of Professional Responsibility', *Anthropology Newsletter*, vol. 27, no. 7 (1984), p. 2

Robb, S. Beware the 'Informed Consent', Editorial, *Nursing Research*, vol. 32, no. 3 (1983), p. 132

Qualitative Approaches

In this section the authors have been selected because of their focus on methodology associated with different research approaches. Research questions, design and the problems of reliability and validity that relate to each approach are explored by different authors. The articles in the first section address the issues related to ethnography. This is followed by sections on the issues and methods of ethnoscience, ethology, ethnomethodology, grounded theory and phenomenology. Specific studies in nursing and the health care field using these approaches are included in the second part of the bibliography.

The Ethnographic Approach

Aamodt, A.M. 'Examining Ethnography for Nurse Researchers', *Western Journal of Nursing Research*, vol. 4, no. 2 (1982), pp. 209-21

Field, P.A. 'Ethnography as a Research Method in Nursing: An Evaluation of the Method' in G. Zilm, A. Hilton and M. Richmond (eds.), *Nursing Research - A Basis for Practice, Service and Education*, Proceedings of the National Nursing Research Conference, University of British Columbia, Vancouver, 1982, pp. 39-47

Frake, C.O. 'The Ethnographic Study of Cognitive Systems' in T. Gladwin and W.C. Sturveant (eds.), *Anthropology and Human Behavior* (Anthropological Society of Washington, Washington, D.C., 1962), pp. 72-85

Hammersley, M. and Atkinson, P. *Ethnography Principles in Practice* (Tavistock Publications, London, 1983)

Kay, M.A. 'Writing an Ethnography of Birth' in M.A. Kay (ed.), *Anthropology of Human Birth* (F.A. Davis Co., Philadelphia, 1982), pp. 1-24

Le Compte, M. and Goertz, J.P. 'Problems of Reliability and Validity in Ethnographic Research', *Review of Educational Research*, vol. 52, no. 1 (1982), pp. 31-60

Owusu, M. 'Ethnography of Africa: The Usefulness of the Useless', *American Anthropologist*, vol. 80 (1978), pp. 310-34

Raggucci, A. 'The Ethnographic Approach to Nursing Research', *Nursing Research*, vol. 21, no. 6 (1972), pp. 485-90

Robertson, H.B. and Boyle, J.S. 'Ethnography: Contributions to Nursing Research', *Journal of Advanced Nursing*, vol. 9, no. 1 (1984), pp. 43-50

Sanday, P.R. 'The Ethnographic Paradigm(s)', *Administrative Science Quarterly*, vol. 24 (1979), pp. 527-38

Weppner, R.S. (ed.) *Street Ethnography: Selected Studies of Crime and Drug Use in Natural Settings* (Sage Publications, Beverly Hills, California, 1977)

Whyte, W.F. *Street Corner Society*, 2nd edn (University of Chicago Press, Chicago, 1955)

Wilson, S. 'The Use of Ethnographic Techniques in Educational Research', *Review of Educational Research*, vol. 47, no. 1 (1977), pp. 245-65

Wolcott, H. 'Criteria for an Ethnographic Approach to Research in Schools', *Human Organization*, vol. 34, no. 2 (1975), pp. 111-28

Ethnoscience

Bush, M.T., Ullrom, J.A. and Osborne, O. 'The Meaning of Mental Health: A Report of Two Ethnoscientific Studies', *Nursing Research*, vol. 24, no. 2 (1975), pp. 130-44

Evaneshko, V. and Kay, M.A. 'The Ethnoscience Research Technique', *Western Journal of Nursing Research*, vol. 4, no. 1 (1982), pp. 49-64

Leininger, M. 'Ethnoscience: A Promising Research Approach to Improve Nursing Practice', *Image: The Journal of Nursing Scholarship*, vol. 3, no. 1 (1969), pp. 2-8

Spradley, J.P. and McCurdy, D. *The Cultural Experience: Ethnography in Complex Society* (Science Research Associates, Chicago, 1972)

Spradley, J.P. *You Owe Yourself a Drunk: An Ethnography of Urban Nomads* (Little, Brown and Company, Boston, 1970)

Werner, O. and Fenton, J. 'Method and Theory in Ethnoscience or Ethnoepistemology' in R. Naroll and R. Cohen (eds.), *A Handbook of Method in Cultural Anthropology* (Columbia University Press, New York, 1973), pp. 537-78

Ethology

Eckman, P. (ed.) *Emotion in the Human Face*, 2nd edn (Cambridge University Press, Cambridge, 1983)

Gould, J.L. *Ethology* (W.W. Norton and Company, London, 1982)

Jones, B.N. (ed.) *Ethological Studies of Child Behavior* (Cambridge University Press, Cambridge, 1972)

Ethnomethodology

Garfinkel, H. *Studies in Ethnomethodology* (Prentice-Hall, Englewood Cliffs, New Jersey, 1967)

Grounded Theory Methodology

Atwood, J.R. (1977) 'A Grounded Theory Approach to the Study of Perimortality Care' in M.V. Batey (ed.), *Communicating Nursing Research: Research in the Bicentennial Year*, vol. 9 (Western Interstate Commission for Higher Education, Boulder, Colorado), pp. 339-50

Glaser, B.G. *Theoretical Sensitivity* (The Sociology Press, Mill Valley, California, 1978)

Glaser, B.G. and Strauss, A.L. *The Discovery of Grounded Theory: Strategies for Qualitative Research* (Aldine Publishing Co., Chicago, 1967)

Simms, L.M. 'The Grounded Theory Approach in Nursing Theory', *Nursing Research*, vol. 30, no. 6 (1981), pp. 356-9

Stern, P.N. 'Grounded Theory Methodology: Its Uses and Processes', *Image*, vol. 12, no. 11 (1980), pp. 20-3

Stern, P.N., Allen, L.M., and Moxley, P.A. 'Qualitative Research: The Nurse as Grounded Theorist', *Health Care for Women International*, Vol. 5, (1984, original work published 1982), pp. 371-385

Turner, B.A. 'Some Practical Aspects of Qualitative Data Analysis: One Way of Organizing the Cognitive Processes Associated with the Generation of Grounded Theory', *Quality and Quantity*, vol. 15 (1981), pp. 225-47

Phenomenological Methodology

Davis, A.J. 'The Phenomenological Approach in Nursing Research' in N. Chaska (ed.), *The Nursing Profession: Views Through the Mist* (McGraw-Hill, New York, 1978), pp. 186-97

Oiler, C. 'The Phenomenology: A Challenge to Experimental Psychology', *Nursing Research*, vol. 31 (1982), pp. 178-81

Omery, A. 'Phenomenology: A Method for Nursing Research', *Advances in Nursing Science*, vol. 5, no. 2 (1983), pp. 49-63

Psathas, C. *Phenomenological Sociology: Issues and Applications* (John Wiley and Sons, New York, 1978)

Rogers, M.F. *Sociology, Ethnomethodology and Experience: A Phenomenological Critique* (Cambridge University Press, Cambridge, 1983)

Van Manen, M. 'Objective Inquiry into Structures of Subjectivity', *Journal of Curriculum Theorizing*, vol. 1, no. 1 (1978), pp. 44-64

Wagner, H.R. *Phenomenology of Consciousness and Sociology of the Life-World: An Introductory Study* (University of Alberta Press, Edmonton, 1983)

Literature Review

These two authors do not discuss the mechanics of writing literature reviews. The first is an example of an article which concludes with hypotheses derived from the literature review. The second, a light hearted article, warns against spending too much time in the library.

Fotopoulos, S., Dintruff, D., Costello, K., and Cook, M. 'Adaptation to Breast Cancer: Attributional Issues' in P.A. Ahmed (ed.), *Living and Dying with Cancer* (Elsevier, New York, 1981), pp. 131-52

Van Gennep, A. 'The Research Topic: Or, Folklore Without End' in A. Dundes (ed.), *The Evil Eye: A Folklore Casebook* (Garland Publishing Company, New York, 1981), pp. 2-9

Entering the Field

Broolen, D. 'Making It In Paradise', *Nursing Research*, vol. 33, no. 6 (1984), p. 318

Process of Data Gathering

The articles and books in this section were selected because of a focus on data gathering methods. There is a selection of references on observation which present approaches, pitfalls and common problems. Dean and Whyte examine the problems of the truthfulness of the information given to the researcher, while Kratz discusses the effect of an observer on an interaction. Gold's classic article identifies the level of participant observation engaged in by the researcher, the roles of the observer are further expanded upon by Pearsall. Robertson looks at the use of participant observation in the work setting. Myers warns of the need to prepare the researcher for the role of observer.

Other articles in this section examine the technical procedures used in stimulated recall, life histories, suicide notes as a data base and writing fieldnotes. Lofland's book is particularly helpful in relating data gathering techniques to data analysis.

Becker, H.S. and Geer, B. 'Participant Observation: The Analysis of Qualitative Field Data' in R. Adams and J. Press (eds.), *Human Organization Research* (Dorrey Press, Homeward, 1960)

Becker, H.S. and Geer, B. 'Participant Observation and Interviewing: A Comparison' in J.G. Manis and B.N. Meltzer (eds.), *Symbolic Interaction: A Reader in Social Psychology* (Allyn and Bacon, Inc., Boston, 1978), pp. 76-82

Conners, R.D. *Using Stimulated Recall in Naturalistic Settings: Some Technical Procedures* (unpublished handbook, Centre for Research in Teaching, Faculty of Education, University of Alberta, Edmonton, 1978)

Dean, J.P. and Whyte, W.F. 'How Do You Know If the Informant is Telling the Truth?', *Human Organization*, vol. 17, no. 2 (1958), pp. 34-8

Gold, R.L. 'Roles in Sociological Observation', *Social Forces*, vol. 36 (1958), pp. 217-23

Gorden, R.L. (1975) *Interviewing: Strategy, Techniques and Tactics* (Dorsey Press, Homewood, Illinois)

Kluckhohn, F.R. 'The Participant-Observer Technique in Small Communities', *American Journal of Sociology*, vol. 46 (1940), pp. 331-43

Kratz, C. 'Participant Observation in Dyadic and Triadic Situations', *International Journal of Nursing Studies*, vol. 12, no. 3 (1975), pp. 169-74

Languess, L.C. *The Life History in Anthropological Science* (Holt, Rinehart and Winston, New York, 1965)

Lester, D. and Reeve, C. 'The Suicide Notes of Young and Old People', *Psychological Reports*, vol. 50 (1982), p. 334

Lofland, J. *Analyzing Social Settings: A Guide to Qualitative Observation and Analysis* (Wadsworth Publishing Company, California, 1971)

McCall, G.J. and Simmonds, J.L. (eds.) *Issues in Participant Observation* (Addison-Wesley Publications, Reading, Massachusetts, 1969)

Myers, J.Z. 'Unleashing the Untrained: Observations on Student Ethnographers' in P.J. Brink (ed.), *Transcultural Nursing: A Book of Readings* (Prentice-Hall, Englewood Cliffs, New Jersey, 1976), pp. 204-13

Pearsall, M. 'Participant Observation as a Role and Method in Behavioral Research', *Nursing Research*, vol. 14, no. 1 (1965), pp. 37-42

Robertson, C.M. 'A Description of Participant Observation of Clinical Teaching', *Journal of Advanced Nursing*, vol. 7, no. 6 (1982), pp. 549-54

Rogoff, B. 'Spot Observation: An Introduction and Examination', *Institute for Comparative Human Development*, vol. 2, no. 2 (1978), pp. 21-6

Spradley, J.P. *The Ethnographic Interview* (Holt, Rinehart and Winston, New York, 1979)

———— *Participant Observation* (Holt, Rinehart and Winston, New York, 1980)

Suelzle, M. and Pasquale, F.L. 'How to Record Observations: Writing Fieldnotes' in L. Borzak (ed.), *Field Study: A Sourcebook for Experiential Learning* (Sage Publications, Beverly Hills, California, 1981), pp. 151-9

Alternative Methods of Data Gathering
In this section authors are included who have written about some alternative methods of data collection. Life histories, case studies and team research are included. Examples of studies using these approaches can be found in the second section of the bibliography.

Case Studies
Kennedy, M.M. 'Generalizing from Single Case Studies', *Evaluation Quarterly*, vol. 3, no. 4 (1979), pp. 661-78

Combined Approaches
Hockey, L. *Women in Nursing* (Hodder and Stoughton, London, 1976)

152   *Bibliography*

Sieber, S.D. 'The Integration of Fieldwork and Survey Methods', *American Journal of Sociology*, vol. 78 (1978), pp. 1335-59

Life History

Bertaux, D. (ed.) *Biography and Society: The Life History Approach to the Social Sciences* (Sage Publications, Beverly Hills, California, 1981)

Languess, L.L. *The Life History in Anthropological Science* (Holt, Rinehart and Winston, New York, 1965)

Team Research

Douglas, J.D. *Investigative Social Research: Individual and Team Research* (Sage Publications, Beverly Hills, California, 1976)

Use of Diaries

Woodham-Smith, C. *Florence Nightingale, 1820-1910* (Atheneum, New York, 1983)

Data Analysis and Report Writing

This section provides additional information on data analysis and reporting of data. Some writers, for example, Bailyn, Berreman, Douglas and Edginton examine some of the theoretical aspects of data analysis, discussing issues related to reliability and validity of both qualitative and quantitative approaches. Fox, Hutchinson, Knafl, Sprout and Turner all examine the practicalities of handling qualitative data. Turner gives some practical advice on procedures for those interested in grounded theory. Podolefsky and McCarty is a useful reference for those wishing to use the computer for sorting and analyzing data.

Lofland and Fuller both provide help in the writing of the report and/or abstract for a qualitative study. This is often a difficult area for the novice researcher and one that is frequently neglected in research books. Some of the articles in the section of the bibliography dealing with validity and reliability may also be helpful when considering data analysis.

Bailyn, L. 'Research as a Cognitive Process: Implications for Data Analysis', *Quality and Quantity*, vol. 11 (1977), pp. 97-117

Berreman, G.D. 'Emic and Etic Analyses in Social Anthropology', *American Anthropologist*, vol. 68 (1966), pp. 346-54

Burling, R. 'Cognition and Componential Analysis: God's Truth or Hocus-Pocus?', *American Anthropologist*, vol. 66 (1964), pp. 20-9

D'Andrade, R.G. 'A Propositional Analysis of U.S. American Beliefs About Illness' in K.H. Basso and H. Selby (eds.), *Meaning in Anthropology* (University of New Mexico Press, Albuquerque, 1976)

Douglas, M. 'Deciphering a Meal', *Daedalus*, vol. 101, no. 1 (1972), pp. 61-81

Edginton, E.S. 'Statistical Inference from N = 1 Experiments', *Journal of Psychology*, vol. 65 (1967), pp. 195-9

Fox, D.J. 'The Analysis of Qualitative Data' in D.J. Fox (ed.), *Fundamentals of Nursing Research*, 3rd edn (Appleton-Century-Crofts, New York, 1976), pp. 259-81

Fuller, E.O. 'Preparing an Abstract of a Nursing Study', *Nursing Research*, vol. 32, no. 5 (1983), pp. 316-7

Goodenough, W.H. 'Componential Analysis', *Science*, vol. 156 (1967), pp. 1203-9

Harris, M. 'Emics, Etics and the New Ethnography' in M. Harris (ed.), *The Rise of Anthropological Theory* (Thomas W. Crowell, New York, 1968)

Hutchinson, S.A. 'Creating Meaning Out of Horror', *Nursing Outlook*, vol. 32, no. 2 (1984), pp. 86-90

Kirk, R.C. 'Microcomputers in Anthropological Research', *Sociological Methods and Research*, vol. 9, no. 4 (1981), pp. 473-92

Knafl, K.A. and Howard, M.J. 'Interpreting and Reporting Qualitative Research', *Research in Nursing and Health*, vol. 7 (1984), pp. 17-24

Lofland, J. 'Styles of Reporting Qualitative Field Research', *American Sociologist*, vol. 9 (1974), pp. 101-11

Melbin, M. 'Mapping Uses and Methods' in R.N. Adams and J.J. Preiss (eds.), *Human Organization Research: Field Relations and Techniques* (Dorsey Press, Homewood, Illinois, 1960), pp. 255-66

Miles, M.B. and Huberman, A.M. *Qualitative Data Analysis: A Source book of New Methods* (Sage Publications, Inc., Beverly Hills, California, 1984)

Podolefsky, A. and McCarty, C. 'Topical Sorting: A Technique for Computer Assisted Data Analysis', *American Anthropologist*, vol. 85, no. 4 (1983), pp. 886-90

Rosengren, K.E. (ed.) (1981) *Advances in Content Analysis*, Sage Publications, Beverly Hills, California

Spradley, J.P. (ed.) *Culture and Cognition: Rules, Maps and Plans* (Chandler Publishing, San Francisco, 1972)

Sproull, L.S. and Sproull, R.F. 'Managing and Analyzing Behavioral Records: Explorations in Nonnumeric Data Analysis', *Human Organization*, vol. 41, no. 4 (1982), pp. 283-90

Swanson, E. and McCloskey, J.C. 'The Manuscript Review Process of Nursing Journals', *Image*, vol. 14, no. 3 (1982), pp. 72-6

Turner, B.A. 'Some Practical Aspects of Qualitative Data Analysis: One Way of Organizing the Cognitive Processes Associated with the Generation of Grounded Theory', *Quality and Quantity*, vol. 15 (1981), pp. 225-47

Van Manen, M. 'Practicing Phenomenological Writing', *Phenomenology + Pedagogy*, vol. 2, no. 1 (1984), pp. 36-9

Issues Related to Validity and Reliability in Qualitative Research
One major field of discussion is the question of reliability and validity in qualitative research. The following authors present a variety of view points and critical appraisal of some anthropological work (De Miele and Noel). Discussion of the role of triangulation for validating observations is presented. Mixing quantitative and qualitative approaches by using survey and fieldwork is discussed by Sieben. These articles should prove thought provoking for those interested in undertaking qualitative studies.

Brace, C.L., Gamble, G.R., and Bond, J.T. *Race and Intelligence: Anthropological Studies No. 8* (American Anthropological Association, Washington, D.C., 1971)

Brady, I. 'Speaking in the Name of the Real: Freeman and Mead on Samoa', *American Anthropologist*, vol. 85 (1983), pp. 908-47

Chapman, C.R. 'Measurement of Pain: Problems and Issues', *Advances in Pain Research and Therapy*, vol. 1 (1976), p. 345

De Miele, R. *Castaneda's Journey* (Capra Press, Santa Barbara, 1976)

Gregory, J.R. 'The Myth of the Male Ethnographer and the Woman's World', *Journal of the American Anthropological Association*, vol. 86, no. 2 (1984), pp. 316-27

Jick, T.D. 'Mixing Qualitative and Quantitative Methods: Triangulation in Action', *Administrative Science Quarterly*, vol. 24 (1979), pp. 602-11

Noel, D. *Seeing Castaneda: Reactions to the 'Don Juan' Writings of Carlos Castaneda* (G.P. Putnam and Sons, New York, 1975)

Scriven, M. 'Objectivity and Subjectivity in Educational Research' in L.G. Thomas (ed.), *Philosophical Direction of Educational Research: The 71st Yearbook of the National Society for the Study of Education* (University of Chicago Press, Chicago, 1972)

Related Readings

Carnevali, D. 'Preoperative Anxiety', *American Journal of Nursing*, vol. 7 (1966), pp. 1536-8

Cohen, H.A. *The Nurse's Quest for a Professional Identity* (Addison-Wesley Publications, Menlo Park, 1981)

Elliott, M.R. 'Maternal Infant Bonding', *Canadian Nurse*, vol. 79, no.8 (1983), pp. 28-31

Gagan, J.M. 'Methodological Notes on Empathy', *Advances in Nursing Science*, vol. 5, no. 2 (1983), pp. 65-72

Klaus, M.H. and Kennell, J.H. *Parent Infant Bonding: The Impact of Early Separation or Loss on Family Development* (C.V. Mosby, St. Louis, 1976)

Leininger, M. *Caring: An Essential Human Need* (Charles B. Slack, New Jersey, 1981)

Orem, D.E. *Nursing: Concepts of Practice*, 2nd edn (McGraw-Hill, New York, 1980)

Roy, Sister C. *Introduction to Nursing: An Adaptation Model* (Prentice-Hall, Englewood Cliffs, New Jersey, 1976)

PART 2: QUALITATIVE STUDIES IN NURSING AND RELATED HEALTH CARE FIELDS

This section of the bibliography presents a selection of qualitative studies that have been conducted in health care related research. The first section is general and consists of exploratory and descriptive studies that have used open-ended interviews of participant observation as the major modes of data gathering. Some researchers used both qualitative measures and instruments, such as attribute scales or other personality measures.

Following the general section studies have been identified and classified according to the qualitative approach that has been employed. Examples of ethnography, ethnology, ethnoscience and grounded theory have been included. Some examples of case studies and multi-site, multiple researcher studies have also been included. It is hoped that the studies selected will provide the beginning researcher with some examples of qualitative studies that will help them to determine whether the question and the approach they have in mind are appropriate.

General

Aamodt, A.A., Grassl-Herwehe, S., Farrell, F., and Hullee, J. Jr. 'The Child's View of Chemically Induced Alopecia' in M. Leininger (ed.), *Care: The Essence of Nursing and Health* (Stark Incorporated, Thorofare, New Jersey, 1984), pp. 217-32

————— *Neighbouring Care and Norwegian-American Women*, paper presented at the Council of Nursing and Anthropology Symposium, The Society of Applied Anthropology Meeting, Ediburgh, Scotland, 1981

Allen, H. ' "Voices of Concern" - A Study of Verbal Communication About patients in a Psychiatric Unit', *Journal of Advanced Nursing*, vol. 6, no. 5 (1981), pp. 355-62

Altschul, A. *Patient-Nurse Interaction* (Monograph No. 3), University of Edinburgh Department of Nursing Studies (Churchill Livingstone, Edinburgh, 1972)

Anderson, J.M. 'The Social Construction of Illness Experience: Families with a Chronically Ill Child', *Journal of Advanced Nursing*, vol. 6, no. 6 (1981), pp. 427-34

Artinian, B.M. 'The Relationship Between Reciprocal Support and Hope in the Bone Marrow Transplant Child' in E. Hamrin (ed.), *Research: A Challenge for Practice, Proceedings of the Workshop of the European Nurse Researchers' First Open Conference* (Uppsala, Sweden, 1983), pp. 140-5

————— 'Becoming a Dialysis Patient' in E. Hamrin (ed.), *Research: A Challenge for Nursing Practice, Proceedings of the Workshop of the European Nurse Researchers' First Open Conference* (Uppsala, Sweden, 1983), pp. 146-51

Field, D. ' "We didn't want him to die on his own" - Nurse's Accounts of Nursing Dying Patients', *Journal of Advanced Nursing*, vol. 9, no. 1 (1984), pp. 59-70

Gotlieb, L. 'Nursing Clients Toward Health: An Analysis of Nursing Interventions', *Nursing Papers*, vol. 13, no. 1 (1981), pp. 24-31

Hayes, V.E. and Knox, J.E. 'The Experience of Stress in Parents of Children Hospitalized with Long-Term Disabilities', *Journal of Advanced Nursing*, vol. 9, no. 4 (1984), pp. 333-42

Hutchison, S.A. 'Creating Meaning Out of Horror', *Nursing Outlook*, vol. 32, no. 2 (1984), pp. 86-90

Katz, M. 'The Relation of Mothers' Roles and Resources to Infant Care in the Outer Fiji Islands' in L. Marshall (ed.), *Infant Care and Feeding in Oceania* (Gordon and Breach, New York, in press)

Kramer, M. *Reality Shock: Why Nurses Leave Nursing* (C.V. Mosby Company, St. Louis, 1974)

Kratz, C.R. *Care of the Long-Term Sick in the Community* (Churchill Livingstone, Edinburgh, 1978)

Luker, K. 'Goal Attainment: A Possible Model for Assessing the Role of the Health Visitor', *Nursing Times*, vol. 74 (1978), pp. 1257-9

Miller, B.F. 'Categories of Self-Care Needs of Ambulatory Patients with Diabetes', *Advanced Journal of Nursing*, vol. 7 (1982), pp. 25-31

Morse, J.M. 'Understanding Lay Perceptions of Health', paper presented to the Council of Nursing and Anthropology at the XI International Congress of Anthropological and Ethnological Sciences, Vancouver, August 20-25, 1983

———— 'Cultural Context of Infant Feeding in Fiji', *Ecology of Food and Nutrition*, vol. 14 (1984), pp. 287-96

————, Harrison, M. and Prowse, M. *Minimal Breastfeeding*, unpublished manuscript, University of Alberta, 1984

———— and Doan, H. *Becoming a Woman: Analysis of Adolescents' Response to Menarche*, paper presented to the Society for Applied Anthropology, Toronto, March 14-18, 1984

Quarnstrom, U. and Lindstrom, C. 'Grief Reaction Following Death of a Significant Other' in E. Hamrin (ed.), *Research: A Challenge for Nursing Practice, Proceedings of the Workgroup of European Nurse Researchers First Open Conference* (Uppsala, Sweden, 1983), pp. 133-9

Soares, C.A. 'Low Verbal Usage and Status Maintenance Among Intensive Care Nurses' in N.L. Chaska (ed.), *The Nursing Profession: Views Through the Mist* (McGraw-Hill, New York, 1978), pp. 198-204

Sudnow, D. *Passing On: The Social Organization of Dying* (Prentice-Hall, Englewood Cliffs, New Jersey, 1967)

Tagliocozzo, D.I. and Mauksch, H.O. 'The Patient's View of the Patient's Role' in J.E. Gartley (ed.), *Patients, Physicians and Illness*, 3rd edn (Collier-MacMillan, London, 1979), pp. 185-201

Thompson, M. 'An Investigation of the Relationship of Love, Mutuality, Freedom and Newness with the Perception of Hope in Patients with the Diagnosis of Cancer', unpublished M.N. thesis, California State University, Los Angeles, 1980

Toohey, S. 'Patient-Nurse Interactions in the Emergency Department: An Exploratory Study', unpublished M.N. thesis, University of Alberta, Edmonton, Alberta, 1984

Wasner, M. 'Health and Nursing: Evolving Once Concept by Involving the Other', *Nursing Papers*, vol. 13, no. 1 (1981), pp. 10-17

Ethnography

Davis, J. 'Teachers, Kids, and Conflict: Ethnography of Junior High School' in J.P. Spradley and D.W. McCurdy (eds.), *Sociological Methods* (Aldine Publications, Chicago, 1972), pp. 103-19

Field, P.A. 'An Ethnography: Four Nurses' Perspectives of Nursing in a Community Setting', unpublished PhD thesis, University of Alberta, 1980

Field, P.A. 'An Ethnography: Four Public Health Nurses' Perspectives of Nursing', *Journal of Advanced Nursing*, vol. 8, no. 1 (1983), pp. 3-12

Germain, C. *The Cancer Unit: An Ethnography* (Nursing Resources Inc., Wakefield, Massachusetts, 1979)

Goffman, E. *Asylums* (Anchor Books, Doubleday and Company, New York, 1961)

Kay, M. *The Anthropology of Human Birth* (F.A. Davis Co., Philadelphia, 1982)

Rosanhan, D.L. 'On Being Sane in Sane Places', *Science*, vol. 179 (1973), pp. 250-8

Weisner, T.S., Gallimore, R., and Thorp, R. 'Concordance Between the Ethnographer Folk Perspectives: Observed Performance and Self-Ascription of Sibling Caretaker Roles', *Human Organization*, vol. 41, no. 3 (1982), pp. 237-44

Ethnoscience

Boyle, J.S. 'Indigenous Caring Practices in a Guatemalan Colonia' in M. Leininger (ed.), *Care: The Essence of Nursing and Health* (Slack Incorporated, New Jersey, 1984), pp. 123-32

Frake, C.O. 'The Diagnosis of Disease Among the Subanun of Mindanao', *American Anthropologist*, vol. 63, no. 1 (1961), pp. 113-32

Moore, M.S.M. 'Self-Care and Caretaking of the Adolescent Asthmatic' in M. Leininger (ed.), *Care: The Essence of Nursing and Health* (Slack Incorporated, New Jersey, 1984), pp. 113-22

Morse, J.M. 'An Ethnoscientific Analysis of Comfort: A Preliminary Investigation', *Nursing Papers*, vol. 15, no. 1 (1983), pp. 6-19

Ray, M.A. 'The Development of A Classification System of Institutional Caring' in M. Leininger (ed.), *Care: The Essence of Nursing and Health* (Slack Incorporated, New Jersey, 1984), pp. 95-112

Ethology

Côté, J. *A Description of the Post-Operative Response of Newborns*, ongoing project, Faculty of Nursing, University of Alberta, Edmonton

Newman, L.F. (1981) 'Social and Sensory Environment of Low Birth Weight Infants in a Special Care Nursery: An Anthropological Investigation', *The Journal of Nervous and Mental Disease*, vol. 169, no. 7, pp. 448-55

Grounded Theory

Fagerhaugh, S. and Strauss, A.L. *Politics of Pain Management* (Addison-Wesley Publications, Menlo Park, California, 1977)

Field, P.A. 'Client Care-Seeking Behaviours in a Community Setting and Their Sources of Satisfaction with Nursing Care', *Nursing Papers*, vol. 14, no. 1 (1982), pp. 15-29

Field, P.A. 'Client Careseeking Behaviours and Nursing Care' in M. Leininger (ed.), *Care: The Essence of Nursing and Health* (J.B. Slack, New Jersey, 1984), pp. 249-62

Glaser, B.G. and Strauss, A.L. *Awareness of Dying* (Aldine Publications, New York, 1966)

———— *Status Passage* (Aldine Publications, New York, 1971)

May, K.A. 'A Typology of Detachment and Involvement Styles Adopted During Pregnancy by First-Time Expectant Fathers', *Western Journal of Nursing Research*, vol. 2, no. 2 (1980), pp. 445-61

May, K.A. 'Three Phases in Development of Father Involvement in Pregnancy', *Nursing Research*, vol. 31, no. 6 (1982), pp. 337-342

Melia, K. ' "Tell It As It Is" - Qualitative Methodology and Nursing Research: Understanding the Nurse's World', *Journal of Advanced Nursing*, vol. 7, no. 4 (1982), pp. 327-36

Melia, K.M. 'Student Nurses' Construction of Occupational Socialization', *Sociology of Health and Illness*, vol. 6, no. 2 (1984), pp. 132-51

Quint, J.Q. *The Nurse and the Dying Patient* (The MacMillan Company, New York, 1967)

Pyles, S.H. and Stern, P.N. 'Discovery of Nursing Gestalt in Critical Care Nursing: The Importance of the Gray Gorilla Syndrome', *Image: The Journal of Nursing Scholarship*, vol. 15, no. 2 (1983), pp. 51-7

Stern, P.N. 'Integrative Discipline in Stepfather Families', PhD dissertation, University of California, San Francisco. *Dissertation Abstracts International*, B, 37 (University Microfilm No. 77-527b)

————— 'Stepfather Families: Integration Around Child Discipline', *Issues in Mental Health Nursing*, vol. 1, no. 2 (1978), pp. 50-6

Wilson, H.S. 'Limiting Intrusion: Social Control of Outsiders in a Healing Community', *Nursing Research*, vol. 26, no. 2 (1977), pp. 103-10

Phenomenology

Benner, P. *From Novice to Expert: Excellence and Power in Clinical Practice* (Addison-Wesley Publications, Menlo Park, 1984)

Buytendijk, F.J. *Pain* (Hutchison and Co., London, 1961)

Field, P.A. 'A Phenomenological Look at Giving an Injection', *Journal of Advanced Nursing*, vol. 6, no. 7 (1981), pp. 291-6

Kelpin, V. 'Birthing Pain', *Phenomenology + Pedagogy*, vol. 2, no. 2 (1984), pp. 178-90

Raffer, S. 'Parental Uncertainty as Pain: A Reading of Dr. Spock', *Phenomenology + Pedagogy*, vol. 1, no. 3 (1983), pp. 335-48

Rollans, B. 'Living the Experience of Old Age Forgetfulness with People for Whom We Care', *Phenomenology + Pedagogy*, vol. 2, no. 2 (1984), pp. 151-62

Van den Berg, J.H. *The Psychology of the Sick Bed* (Duquesne University Press, Pittsburgh, 1966)

Case Studies

Becker, H.S., Geer, B., Hughes, E.C. and Strauss, A.L. *Boys in White: Student Culture in Medical School* (University of Chicago Press, Chicago, 1961)

Dingwall, R. *The Social Organization of Health Visitor Training* (Croom Helm Ltd., London, 1977)

Geer, B., Haas, J. Vivona, C., Miller, S.J., Woods C. and Becker, H.S. 'Learning the Ropes: Situational Learning in Four Occupational Training Programs' in I. Deutscher and E.J. Thompson (eds.), *Among the People: Encounters with the Poor* (Basic Books Inc., New York, 1968), pp. 209-33

Gow, K.M. *How Nurses' Emotions Affect Patient Care: Self-Studies by Nurses* (Springer Publishing Company, New York, 1982)

Koos, E.L. *The Health of Regionville: What the People Thought and Did About It* (Columbia University Press, New York, 1954; Hafner Ltd., New York, 1967, revised)

Larsen, J. 'A Psychosocial Study of the Career Development of Selected Nurses with Earned Doctoral Degrees', unpublished PhD thesis, Faculty of Education, University of Alberta, 1984

Perkins, E.R. *Education for Childbirth and Parenthood* (Croom Helm Ltd., London, 1980)

Multi-Site Study Using Observation and Interview
Degner, L.F., Beaton, J.T. and Glass, H.P. *Life-Death Decision Making in Health Care: A Descriptive Study* (University of Manitoba School of Nursing, Winnipeg, 1981)

Habenstein, R.W. and Christ, E.A. *Professionalizer, Traditionalizer and Utilizer* (University of Missouri, Columbus, 1955). Open-Ended Interviews, Multi-Site Research (10 hospitals), Personal Inventory and Tasks Attitude Schedule

Rosenthal, C.J., Marshall, R.W., MacPherson, A.S. and French, S.E. *Nurses, Patients and Families* (Croom Helm, London, 1980)

Multiple Methods
Coser, R.L. *Life in the Ward* (Michigan State University Press, East Lansing, 1962). [Participant observation and interviews.]

Levinson, D.J. and Gallagher, E.B. *Patienthood in the Mental Hospital* (Houghton Mifflin Company, Boston, 1964). [Participant observation and the patient-role conception. Inventory developed from observations, then used in second part of study.]

Maloni, J.A. 'The Birthing Room: Some Insights into Parents' Experiences' in L.H. Sherwen and C. Toussic-Weingarten (eds.), *Analysis Applications of Nursing Research: Parent-Neonate Studies* (Wadsworth Health Sciences Division, Monterrey, California, 1983), pp. 142-155. [Interviews and attitude scales]

Morse, J.M. 'Descriptive Analysis of Cultural Coping Mechanisms Utilized for the Reduction of Parturition Pain and Anxiety in Fiji', *Dissertation Abstracts International*, vol. 42, no. 11 (1982), pp. 4363B-4364B (University Microfilms No. 8202200)

AUTHOR INDEX

SUBJECT INDEX

Abstract
  components, 34
  example, 37-39
Analytic sociology definition, 27

Bias
  in field notes, 80
  literature review, 34
  open-ended interview, 35
  sample selection, 35
Budget
  example, 43
  preparing, 40

Cameras, 59, 61
  types of, 61
Card sorts, 107
  diadic, 107
  triadic, 107
  q-sorts, 107
Case studies, 87-88
  of historical organizations, 88
Cases, 106
Categories, 9
  atypical, 106
  negative, 106
Classification systems (see Taxonomy), 104
Coding, 97, 99
  color, 101
  definition, 137
  methods, 99-101
Concepts
  deductive theory, 4
  definition, 2, 137
  factor-isolating theory, 8
  grounded theory, 6
  maturity, 14
Conceptual framework
  definition, 4, 137
Confidentiality, 52-53
Consent
  implied, 44
  of guardian, 46
  ongoing, 46
  parental, 46
  photographs, 47
  verbal, 44

  withdrawal, 46
  written, 44
Consent form
  components, 42
  example, 45
Constant comparison, 113
Construct, 4, 12, 137
Content analysis, 103
  latent, 103
  manifest, 103
  types, 103
Context
  lateral, 87
  lineal, 87
  social, 117
Cover page
  components, 37
  example, 36

Data
  analysis, 96
  final analysis, 122
  gathering, 59-62
  hard, 12
  organization, 129-130
  rich, 72
  soft, 11
  types, 11-12
Data analysis, 91-124
  coding, 97
  phase analysis, 103
  semantic analysis, 103
  static analysis, 103
Data filing systems, 101-103
  computerized, 102-103
  manual methods, 101-102
  methods, 101
Deduction, 137
Deductive theory
  definition, 2, 136-137
  limitations, 2, 15
  purpose, 4
  strengths, 5
Diadic card sort, 107
Diary
  informant, 85

165

relationships with, 54
role of, 58
secondary, 59
types of, 57-58
Informed consent
components, 42
definition, 42
photographs, 47
procedures, 52-53
requirements, 42, 44
special populations, 46
types, 44
Interviewing
order of questions, 70
pitfalls, 67-73
Interviews
guided, 16, 65, 67
open-ended, 16, 65-67
pitfalls, 67-73
structured, 16
superficial, 72
techniques, 65-73
telephone, 69
Investigators
multiple, 53, 88
responsibility, 72, 73

Knowledge
common sense, 19

Latent content analysis, 103
Lateral context, 87
Lexeme, 138
Life history, 84-85
method, 84-85
use of photographs, 85
purpose, 84
tape recorded, 85
'Life world' phenomena, 20
Lineal context, 87
Literature review
approaches, 34
writing, 39

Manifest content analysis, 103
Matrix formulation, 104
Maps
use of, 82, 84
Meaning, 67
definition, 19
explicit, 66
implicit, 66
Methods
case studies, 87-88
describing, 39

mixing, 15-16
multiple, 15-16
official documents, 86
participant observation, 75-79
personal collections, 86
qualitative (definition), 138
quantitative (definition), 138
selecting, 13-14, 29
Moral
dilemma, 47-49
Multiple site research, 88

Negative cases, 106
'New ethnography', 21

Observational techniques, 75-79
ethical considerations, 78-79
problems, 78-79
setting, 77
spot observations, 78
types, 76-77
One-way mirror, 77
Open-ended interview, 65-67
construction, 74
Organizations
access, 51
clearance, 51-52
Outline, 130, 131

Paradigm, 4, 138
Participant, 138
Participant mortality, 119
Participant observation
bias in, 76
complete observer, 77
complete participation, 76
entry, 54-56
ethical considerations, 76
fieldnotes, 76
'going native', 76
involvement in setting, 53
observer-as-participant, 77
one-way mirrors, 77
participant-as-observer, 76
problems, 78-79
setting, selecting, 77
types of, 76-77
use of, 21
Phenomenology
approaches, 27-28
definition, 21, 138
examples, 28-29
philosophy, 28
question, 27
styles of writing, 130